Jane Eyre

by Charlotte Brontë

Michael Jones

Series Editors:
Sue Bennett and Dave Stockwin

HODDER EDUCATION
AN HACHETTE UK COMPANY

The Publishers would like to thank the following for permission to reproduce copyright material.

Photo credits

p. 9 AF archive/Alamy; **p. 13** The Keasbury-Gordon Photograph Archive/Alamy; **p. 18** oben901/Fotolia; **p. 24** Moviestore Collection/Rex; **pp. 26, 42** Focus/Everett/Rex; **p. 50** 20th Century Fox/The Kobal Collection; **p. 53** AF archive/Alamy; **p. 61** Moviestore Collection/Rex

Orders: please contact Bookpoint Ltd, 130 Park Drive, Milton Park, Abingdon, Oxon OX14 4SE. Telephone: (44) 01235 827720. Fax: (44) 01235 400454. Email education@bookpoint.co.uk Lines are open from 9 a.m. to 5 p.m., Monday to Saturday, with a 24-hour message answering service. You can also order through our website: www.hoddereducation.co.uk

ISBN: 978 1 4718 5360 9

First published in 2016 by

Hodder Education,

An Hachette UK Company

Carmelite House

50 Victoria Embankment

London EC4Y 0DZ

www.hoddereducation.co.uk

Impression number 10 9 8 7 6 5 4 3 2 1

Year 2020 2019 2018 2017 2016

Cover photo © Lynn Koenig/Getty Images

Illustrations by Integra Software Services Pvt. Ltd.

Typeset in Bliss Light 11/13 by Integra Software Services Pvt. Ltd., Pondicherry, India

Printed in Italy

A catalogue record for this title is available from the British Library.

Contents

Getting the most from this guide

This guide is designed to help you raise your achievement in your examination response to *Jane Eyre*. It is intended for you to use throughout your GCSE English literature course. It will help you when you are studying the novel for the first time and also during your revision.

The following features have been used throughout this guide to help you focus your understanding of the novel.

Target your thinking

A list of **introductory questions** labelled by Assessment Objective is provided at the beginning of each chapter to give you a breakdown of the material covered. They target your thinking in order to help you work more efficiently by focusing on the key messages.

Build critical skills

These boxes offer an opportunity to consider some **more challenging questions**. They are designed to encourage deeper thinking, analysis and exploratory thought. Building and practising critical skills in this way will give you a real advantage in the examination.

GRADE *FOCUS*

It is possible to know a novel well and yet still underachieve in the examination if you are unsure of what the examiners are looking for. The **GRADE FOCUS** boxes give a clear explanation of **how you may be assessed**, with an emphasis on the criteria for gaining a Grade 5 and a Grade 8.

REVIEW YOUR LEARNING

At the end of each chapter you will find this section to **test your knowledge**: a series of short, specific questions to ensure that you have understood and absorbed the key messages of the chapter. Answers to the 'Review your learning' questions are provided in the final section of the guide (p. 108).

GRADE *BOOSTER*

Read and remember these pieces of helpful **grade-boosting advice.** They provide top tips from experienced teachers and examiners who can advise you on what to do, as well as what *not* to do, in order to maximise your chances of success in the examination.

Key quotation

Key quotations are highlighted for you, so that if you wish you may use them as **supporting evidence** in your examination answers. Further quotations, grouped by characterisation, theme and the author's methods, can be found in the 'Top quotations' section on page 102 of the guide. All page references in this guide refer to the 2006 edition of *Jane Eyre*, published by Penguin Classics (ISBN 9780141441146).

'Reader, I married him.'
(p. 517)

Introduction

Studying the text

You may find it useful to dip into this guide in sections as and when you need them, rather than reading it from start to finish. For example, the section on 'Context' can be read before you read the novel itself, since it offers an explanation of the relevant historical, cultural and literary background to the text. In 'Context' you will find information about aspects of Charlotte Brontë's life and times that influenced her writing; the particular issues with which she was concerned; and where the novel stands in terms of the literary tradition to which it belongs.

The relevant 'Plot and structure' sections in this guide could be helpful to you either before or after you read each chapter of *Jane Eyre*. As well as a summary of events there is also commentary on the author's methods, so that you are aware of both the key events and the literary features in each part of the novel. Later, the sections on 'Characterisation', 'Themes' and 'Language, style and analysis' will help develop your thinking further, in preparation for written responses on particular aspects of the text.

Many students also enjoy the experience of being able to bring something extra to their classroom lessons in order to be 'a step ahead of the game'. Alternatively, you may have missed a classroom session or feel that you need a clearer explanation, and the guide can help you with this too.

An initial reading of the section on 'Assessment Objectives and skills' will enable you to make really effective notes in preparation for your written answers, because you will have a very clear understanding of what the examiners are looking for. The Assessment Objectives are what examination boards base their mark schemes on. In this section the AOs are broken down and clearly explained.

Revising the text

Whether you study the novel in a block of time close to the exam or much earlier in your GCSE English literature course, you will need to revise thoroughly if you are to achieve the very best grade that you can.

Reading this guide should, of course, never be a substitute for reading *Jane Eyre* itself, but it can help. You should first remind yourself of what happens in the novel, and for this the chapter on 'Plot and structure' might be revisited in the first instance. You might then look at the 'Assessment Objectives and skills' section to ensure that you understand what the examiners are, in general, looking for.

'Tackling the exams' then gives you useful information on the exams and on question format, depending on which examination board specification you are following, as well as advice on the examination format, and practical considerations such as the time available for the question and the Assessment Objectives that apply to it.

Advice is also supplied on how to approach the question, writing a quick plan, and 'working' with the text, since all of the examination boards use an extract-based question for *Jane Eyre*. The Charlotte Brontë question is in two parts (only OCR provides an alternative, essay-type question): you will be given an extract from *Jane Eyre* and asked to write in detail about that extract, before being asked to write about an aspect in the novel as a whole. Focused advice on how you might improve your grade follows, and you need to read this section carefully.

You will find examples of exam-style responses in the 'Sample essays' section, with an examiner's comments in the margins so that you can see clearly how to move towards a Grade 5, and how then to move from a Grade 5 to a Grade 8. When looking at the sample answers, bear in mind that the way they are assessed is similar (but not identical) across the boards. It is sensible to look online at the sample questions and materials from the particular board that you are taking, and to try planning answers to as many questions as possible. You might also have fun inventing and answering additional questions, since you can be sure that the ones in the sample materials will not be the ones you see when you open the exam paper!

This guide should help you to clarify your thinking about the novel, but it is not a substitute for your thoughtful reading and discussion of *Jane Eyre*. The guide should also help you consolidate your approach to writing well under the pressure of the examination. The suggestions in the guide can help you to develop habits of planning and writing answers that take the worry out of *how* you write, and so enable you to concentrate on *what* you write.

The guide is intended to complement the work you do with your teacher, not to replace it. At the end of the main sections there are 'Review your learning' questions to support your thinking. There are 'Build critical skills' and 'Grade booster' boxes at various points; these help you to develop the critical and analytical skills you need to achieve a higher grade. There is also a 'Top quotations' section, for characters, themes and the author's methods. Now that all GCSE literature examinations are 'closed book', this 'Top quotations' section will prove helpful in offering you the opportunity to learn short quotations to support points about characters, themes and Charlotte Brontë's methods, as well as being a revision aid.

When writing about the novel, use this guide as a springboard to develop your own ideas. You should not read this guide in order to memorise chunks of it, ready to regurgitate in the exam. Examiners are not looking for set responses: identical answers are dull. They would like to see that you have used everything you have been taught – including by this guide – as a starting point for your own thinking. The examiners hope to reward you for perceptive thought, individual appreciation and varying interpretations. Try to show that you have engaged with the themes and ideas in the novel and that you have explored Charlotte Brontë's methods with an awareness of the context in which she wrote. Above all, don't be afraid to make it clear that you have enjoyed the novel.

When reading *Jane Eyre*

Keep in mind when the novel was written. *Jane Eyre: An Autobiography* was a sensation when it was published in 1847. It was claiming to be the autobiography of a woman called Jane Eyre, edited by a man called Currer Bell (Charlotte Brontë chose to publish under a man's name because in the 1840s attitudes to women writers were so negative). In fact it was a work of fiction written wholly by Charlotte Brontë, but it does draw on aspects of her own life and character. You will recognise elements from other types of writing as well as autobiography. These include romance, mystery, Gothic horror and the coming-of-age novel (or *Bildungsroman*), which tracks the emotional and spiritual development of a young person.

Think of *Jane Eyre* as a novel in the style of an autobiography with a chronological and geographical structure. Each new stage of Jane's development towards maturity either starts or ends with a journey.

The novel is the story of a passionate young woman's social, sexual and spiritual development, but *Jane Eyre* was also a criticism of what Charlotte Brontë called 'the warped system of things' – religious hypocrisy, social pretensions and attitudes towards women. Look out for Charlotte Brontë's critical, satirical and political presentation of a society that offered women fewer opportunities than it offered men.

The novel has distinct elements that would have been recognised at the time as 'Gothic': notice when and how Charlotte Brontë creates a deliberately mysterious and macabre atmosphere, especially around the hidden figure of Bertha at Thornfield Hall.

Watching *Jane Eyre*

Jane Eyre has been adapted as a film many times and in different languages. As long as you remember that you are being examined on the book itself, not on a film version of it, you might gain insights from the ways different directors have interpreted the novel. Famous film adaptations include the 1943 version starring Orson Welles, and the 1996 film by Zeffirelli with a remarkable cast. Recent adaptations include a

2006 four-part BBC television version, available on DVD, and a 2011 film, starring Michael Fassbender and Judi Dench. Radio adaptations leave greater scope for your imagination but these are not as easy to obtain as are audiobooks, which are closer to the original text.

▲ Jane and Mr Rochester in the 1996 film adaptation

Examining the text

You will be examined on Charlotte Brontë's text, so it is important for you to examine the text for yourself. The exam questions are really about Charlotte Brontë as a novelist, and the text of *Jane Eyre* is what you have to use as evidence for what you say.

As you get to know *Jane Eyre* better, ask yourself a series of questions about Charlotte Brontë's reasons for writing each episode as she did:

1. Why did Charlotte Brontë include this episode at this point?
2. What methods did Charlotte Brontë choose to present this episode?
3. How does this episode contribute to the development of the plot?
4. What do we learn about the characters from this part of the novel?
5. What mental images are conjured up by the words? How do they link with images and ideas from elsewhere?
6. How might Charlotte Brontë have expected her readers to react to this episode?
7. What aspects of this part of the novel have relevance today?
8. How effective do you think Charlotte Brontë was in conveying her intentions to her readers?

9 What would be lost if this episode did not exist?
10 What are your personal thoughts about this part of the novel?

And finally...

Jane Eyre is a love story, but not just a love story: it presents personal love and passion, but does so in the context of major ideas of the time, such as religion, education, the structure of society and the freedom of the individual.

Enjoy reading the novel, use the guide to help you as you study the text, and good luck in your exam.

Context

Target your thinking

- What do examiners mean by 'context'? (**AO3**)
- How can awareness of the personal, historical and literary context deepen your understanding of *Jane Eyre*? (**AO3**)
- How might readers in different times see different ideas and issues in the novel? (**AO3**)

What is meant by context?

'Context' (AO3) in GCSE English literature is a wide-ranging term. It has five different aspects:

- **The personal context:** how Charlotte Brontë's life influenced her work.
- **The historical context:** how the time in which the novel was written relates to the ideas and events in *Jane Eyre*.
- **The literary context:** how Charlotte Brontë's own reading influenced the novel.
- **The context of the text:** the time and place within which the text itself is set.
- **The reader context:** the ways in which reader responses reflect different times and places.

GCSE examiners do not want you to reel off information about Charlotte Brontë's life and times. What they are interested in is how your knowledge of her life and times influences your understanding of the novel.

The life of Charlotte Brontë

1816 Charlotte is born on 21 April, the third child of Patrick Brontë and Maria Branwell.

1820 Her father becomes curate in Haworth, a remote village on the Pennine moors in West Yorkshire.

1821–23 Charlotte's mother dies. Charlotte and her siblings are cared for by their uncaring (but very religious) maiden aunt. The Brontë children are free to roam the moors, and to read whatever interests them.

1824 Mr Brontë sends his four eldest daughters to a school for the daughters of poor clergymen at Cowan Bridge. Charlotte's

GRADE BOOSTER

Gaining some knowledge of Charlotte Brontë's life as well as the context of the novel will help you to understand the author's purposes and concerns, as well as any contemporary issues that may have affected the presentation of characters or themes. It's important, however, to avoid simply 'bolting on' biographical or cultural details – they must always be relevant to the question you are answering.

	two eldest sisters, Maria and Elizabeth, die there of tuberculosis.
1825–30	The remaining Brontë children live at Haworth and collaboratively create a complete imaginary world, called Angria.
1831–34	Charlotte attends school at Roe Head.
1835–41	Charlotte returns to Roe Head in 1835 as a governess. This is followed by two other posts as a governess, which she hates.
1841–43	Charlotte, now 26, enrols at the Pensionnat Heger in Brussels, to improve her teaching qualifications in French and to learn German. She falls passionately in love with the married headmaster at the school, Monsieur Heger.
1843	Charlotte tries and fails to open a school in Haworth.
1846	The sisters together publish a book of poems under pseudonyms. Anne's *Agnes Grey* and Emily's *Wuthering Heights* are both accepted by publishers, but Charlotte's partially autobiographical account of her experiences in Brussels, *The Professor*, is rejected. Undeterred, she begins writing *Jane Eyre*.
1847	*Jane Eyre: An Autobiography* is published under the name of Currer Bell, bringing Charlotte the sum of £500.
1848	The 'Bells' find instant fame, once their true identity is known, but Emily and Branwell Brontë die that year.
1849	Charlotte is shattered emotionally when Anne dies of tuberculosis, but publishes *Shirley*.
1853	*Villette,* based on Charlotte's experiences in Brussels, is published.
1854	Charlotte finally (and rather unromantically) marries her father's curate, Arthur Nicholls.
1855	Charlotte becomes pregnant, but dies of pneumonia at the age of 38.

The personal context

This refers to how what was happening in her personal world might have influenced how Charlotte Brontë wrote *Jane Eyre*.

Jane Eyre is not Charlotte Brontë. We cannot simply assume that events in the novel are there because something similar happened to the writer. Nevertheless, as you would expect, authors draw on what they know or have experienced. Various aspects of Jane's life are close to Charlotte Brontë's, but some are closer than others. Below are comments on parts of the novel that link Jane's experiences with her creator's, however tenuous that link may be.

Family

Charlotte Brontë's time as a child in the charge of her unsympathetic, rigid and deeply religious Aunt Branwell may have influenced the way in which she wrote about Jane's unhappy time as a dependant at Gateshead Hall. Charlotte Brontë's highly intelligent sister Maria died at Cowan Bridge School (Lowood School in the novel) and was probably the model for Helen Burns. Reverend Brontë, Charlotte's father, was losing his sight by the time Charlotte was writing *Jane Eyre*, so she wrote of Rochester's blindness with experience of how blindness could change a life. Charlotte also knew of a family called the Eyres, whose house contained a mad relative.

▲ Charlotte Brontë

Education

Lowood School is clearly based on the Cowan Bridge School for the daughters of the clergy that Charlotte and her sisters attended. Maria and Elizabeth Brontë died there of tuberculosis.

Charlotte, like Jane, was a governess, but to Charlotte being a governess was like 'slavery'. The savage satirical portrayal of Blanche Ingram, with her sneering contempt for governesses, is a reflection of Charlotte's attitude to those who employed governesses.

Build critical skills

How does Charlotte Brontë's use of dialogue here show how Jane feels about life at Lowood School after she has been shamed by Mr Brocklehurst?

'"Helen, why do you stay with a girl whom everybody believes to be a liar?"

"Everybody, Jane? Why, there are only eighty people who have heard you called so, and the world contains hundreds of millions."

"But what have I to do with millions? The eighty I know despise me."

"Jane, you are mistaken: probably not one in the school either despises or dislikes you; many, I am sure, pity you much."

"How can they pity me after what Mr Brocklehurst said?"

"Mr Brocklehurst is not a god."'

(p. 82)

Romance and marriage

Charlotte went as a student and a student-teacher to Brussels, where she became infatuated with her teacher, M. Heger. Like Mr Rochester, he was an older man.

During her life Charlotte turned down two offers of marriage and once wrote that if she ever married, she must have an 'intense attachment'. That is certainly Jane's attitude too, since she says at one point, 'My future husband was becoming to me my whole world.' Jane refuses St John because she despises his idea of love.

The historical context

This refers to how what was happening in the wider world might have influenced how Charlotte Brontë wrote *Jane Eyre*.

The position of women

Key quotation

'Women feel just as men feel; they need exercise for their faculties, and a field for their efforts as much as their brothers do.'
(pp. 129–130)

Key quotation

'I am a free human being with an independent will, which I now exert to leave you.'
(p. 293)

When Charlotte Brontë grew up in the first part of the nineteenth century, women were very much second-class citizens. They did not have the vote, in legal terms they were virtually their husband's or father's property, and career opportunities for women – apart from teaching or becoming a governess – hardly existed. This was brought home quite painfully to Charlotte at the age of 20 when she sent some poems to Robert Southey, an established poet, for comment. He told her that 'Literature cannot be the business of a woman's life; and it ought not to be', since (in his view) a woman should be engaged in 'her proper duties' of looking after a home.

It was therefore a bold declaration on Charlotte Brontë's part (using Jane as her mouthpiece or 'persona') to write on behalf of women that 'Women feel just as men feel; they need exercise for their faculties, and a field for their efforts as much as their brothers do' (pp. 129–130). Jane's inheritance eventually gives her a freedom denied to many other women, but earlier she sets a strong example by refusing to let others, even Rochester or St John, decide her life for her: at a moment of most intense love for Rochester she resists his embrace.

Religion

Key quotation

Helen Burns: 'I believe; I have faith; I am going to God.'
(p. 97)

Religion was important for most people in the early nineteenth century and it features significantly in *Jane Eyre*. Charlotte Brontë's father was a moderate clergyman on the evangelical wing of the Church of England, who voiced public opposition to an act of parliament that meant misery for textile workers (the Poor Law Amendment Act 1834). Her father was on the tolerant wing of the Evangelical movement, but her Aunt Branwell, who brought Charlotte up, was a fiercely intolerant Calvinist, who believed that some people were destined for heaven but others for hell. Charlotte also met Roman Catholicism when she was in Brussels, but she seems to have had little sympathy for any kind of religious extremism, Anglican, Catholic or Evangelical.

In the preface to the second edition of *Jane Eyre*, Charlotte Brontë offered a robust defence of her treatment of religion in the novel, stating that, 'Conventionality is not morality. Self-righteousness is not religion. To attack the first is not to assail the last.' She went on to declare that, 'appearance should not be mistaken for truth; narrow human doctrines, that only tend to elate and magnify a few, should not be substituted for the world-redeeming creed of Christ.'

Key quotation

Jane: 'I will keep the law given by God; sanctioned by man.' (p. 365)

Social class

The time in which *Jane Eyre* was written was one of considerable social and political uncertainty. The social structure was much more rigid than today and the gap between rich and poor was even wider, but Britain's ruling classes still remembered the French Revolution of 1789–99, when the French royal family and many aristocrats had been guillotined: they feared a British equivalent. The Brontë children would have heard about the Luddite riots in Yorkshire in 1812, near where their father lived, which were when workers, fearing that the introduction of new machinery would cost them their livelihoods, attacked mill owners. There had also been a massacre of peaceful protesters at St Peter's fields in Manchester when Charlotte Brontë was a child (the Peterloo Massacre of 1819), and as recently as 1831 there had been serious riots in Bristol in which the centre of the city was set aflame. The so-called Great Reform Act of 1832 had removed some of the abuses of elections and given the vote to more middle-class men, but all women and the majority of working men remained excluded. Charlotte Brontë would have known that Chartism, a working-class movement that sought votes for all men (but not women), had widespread support.

Build critical skills

What does Blanche Ingram's view of governesses – 'half of them are detestable and the rest ridiculous' – suggest about Charlotte Brontë's opinion of her and the other upper-class guests at Thornfield?

The ruling classes tended to feel that people should know their place in society – and should stay there. They believed, or claimed to believe, that the social order was the result of God's will and that therefore they had to remain rich and important while others scraped a living as best they could without complaining. No wonder *Jane Eyre*, with its obvious contempt for the pretensions of the rich and the religious, was seen as dangerous! Blanche Ingram is revealed as haughty and superficial; John Reed is selfish, stupid and debauched; Georgiana Reed is vacuous and vain; Eliza Reed is self-absorbed and dislikes human beings.

Rochester has no time or respect for social conventions, but Jane's quiet determination to do only what she (as opposed to her 'betters') believes is right is subtly more subversive. This was particularly so since she started off as a penniless orphan 'dependant' and finished up as a rich woman married to a man of aristocratic rank. Charlotte Brontë shows us Jane valuing people according to their qualities rather than their rank:

the high-ranking guests at Thornfield are shown up as moral pygmies, but someone like Bessie, a mere servant at Gateshead Hall, emerges as more deserving of a reader's respect than any of her employers.

There are times in the novel when Jane's tone and attitude are presented in a way that modern readers might find disturbing, as in the passage below where young Jane is asked whether she would want to leave Gateshead Hall to live with 'poor, low relations called Eyre':

> '"No; I should not like to belong to poor people," was my reply.
>
> "Not even if they were kind to you?"
>
> I shook my head: I could not see how poor people had the means of being kind; and then to learn to speak like them, to adopt their manners, to be uneducated, to grow up like one of the poor women I saw sometimes nursing their children or washing their clothes at the cottage doors of the village of Gateshead: no, I was not heroic enough to purchase liberty at the price of caste.'
>
> (p. 30)

GRADE BOOSTER

To achieve high grades you need to show that you understand how contemporary issues in nineteenth-century society - particularly those of education, the place of women, and the nature of religious behaviour and belief - feature strongly in the novel.

This is put into the mouth of a child, and does not necessarily reflect Charlotte Brontë's own views, since the passage also says: 'I reflected. Poverty looks grim to grown people; still more so to children ... poverty for me was synonymous with degradation' (p. 29). One clue to the author's view is in the reference to the 'poor' Eyre family, since the Eyres prove to be both rich and respectable, emphasising that people should be valued for their personal qualities rather than their wealth or social position.

As readers we do not think better of Mrs Fairfax when she says Leah and John are 'only servants, and one can't converse with them on terms of equality; one must keep them at due distance for fear of losing one's authority' (p. 115). Jane has become 'quite a lady' but as a governess she lives in a no-woman's land that Charlotte Brontë had experienced: neither a member of the family nor an ordinary servant. Victorian society was often suspicious of governesses because they could bring a dangerous sexuality into the family and undermine (as Jane does) the boundaries between governess and the upper-class family.

Key quotation

Jane usually feels 'as if he were my relation rather than my master' (p. 171)

The relationship between Jane and Rochester challenges conventional class attitudes. In the conversation prior to their betrothal, Rochester (cruelly) harps on about Jane's status and need for employment before declaring his love for her. More significant as an indication of his attitudes is when he declares, 'Station! station! – your station is in my heart, and on the necks of those who would insult you, now or hereafter' (p. 304).

The literary context

Stories and poetry are almost as old as human society, but novels have not been around forever. When Charlotte Brontë was writing, the novel was an established but still comparatively new art form.

Charlotte Brontë read widely. What she had read included 'Gothic' novels, the works of Sir Walter Scott and Mary Shelley, and much romantic poetry, especially Byron. She will have known that her own novel, *Jane Eyre*, was part of a tradition of Gothic novels – which had great houses with strange secrets, madness, mysterious events and an eerie atmosphere in which vampire-like figures prowled dark corridors. She also knew that the central male figure, Rochester, would remind readers of romantic Lord Byron, the damaged and dangerous darling of women in the early part of the nineteenth century. The (allegedly) autobiographical approach was a familiar literary device, but what was new was Charlotte's Brontë's intensity of focus on an individual woman, who tells her own story of the battle she faces between her passion and her conscience.

Readers of the time expected novels to be 'realistic' and *Jane Eyre* is realistic in many ways. It creates a recognisable world in which the power of the upper classes determines what lives are possible for others. It recognises that a life without money, as when Jane wanders penniless after leaving Thornfield, is almost impossible. The novel is not just 'realistic', however: it offers a satirical perspective on selfish and hypocritical people like Mrs Reed or Mr Brocklehurst. These characters do not finally thrive: they pay the penalty for their nastiness in a way that does not necessarily happen in life. *Jane Eyre* also has unrealistic – almost magical – happenings, such as Jane hearing Rochester's cry although she is many miles away, and it uses symbolism (e.g. the horse-chestnut tree), not just realism, to tell the story.

GRADE BOOSTER

To achieve the highest grades it is important to draw on the literary context for *Jane Eyre* as well as on the more obvious historical context. The literary context includes poetry as well as fiction, and Charlotte Brontë was consciously writing within and beyond the tradition of Gothic novels.

Key quotation

Mr Brocklehurst: 'Humility is a Christian grace' (p. 41)

The context of the text

The setting for *Jane Eyre* is the north of England, with most of the locations being in remote areas. Charlotte Brontë was familiar with such settings, as she lived most of her life at Haworth, a village on the Pennine moors in West Yorkshire. As in many of the Gothic novels Charlotte had read, much of the central action takes place in a large mansion with a mysterious secret: Thornfield Hall. Other locations are a smaller mansion, Gateshead Hall, the school at Lowood, Moor House and the village of Morton, and finally, the modest manor house of Ferndean. The countryside, where the weather is a permanently significant factor, matters more than any town or city context.

▲ Haworth, on the Pennine moors, where Brontë spent most of her life

GRADE FOCUS

Grade 5

To achieve a Grade 5, students need to show a clear understanding of the contexts in which the novel was written.

Grade 8

To achieve a Grade 8, students need to make perceptive, critical comments about the ways that contextual factors affect the choices that the writer makes.

GRADE BOOSTER

To achieve high grades you need to show that you understand that readers in different times will respond in different ways to the novel's content, style and ideas. *Jane Eyre* was immediately successful and was rapidly reprinted. Most early readers responded positively to the exploration of an individual's thoughts and feelings, but some felt that the book was 'anti-Christian' and others that it was 'improper'. Today, readers recognise that Charlotte Brontë was radical in challenging some of the dominant attitudes of her time, particularly regarding the status and treatment of women.

REVIEW YOUR LEARNING

(Answers are given on p. 108.)

1. What is meant by the term 'context'?
2. Which school was the original for Lowood?
3. Who was Helen Burns based on?
4. What was the occupation of Charlotte Brontë's father?
5. Apart from teaching, what job did Charlotte Brontë have?
6. What view of rich people comes through the novel?
7. What impression do you have of Charlotte Brontë's attitude to religion?
8. How did the way that Jane Eyre is presented as a woman challenge contemporary attitudes to women?
9. What characterises 'Gothic' writing?
10. Is Jane's view of the working classes the same as Charlotte Brontë's?

Plot and structure

Target your thinking

- What are the main events of the novel? (**AO1**)
- How are these events presented by the author? (**AO2**)
- How does Charlotte Brontë use structure in telling the story? (**AO2**)

Plot

Jane Eyre is a novel in the style of an autobiography with a chronological and geographical structure. Jane's emotional and spiritual journey through each of the places below is followed by or started with an actual journey:

1. Gateshead Hall
2. Lowood School
3. Thornfield
4. Gateshead Hall (revisited)
5. Marsh End/Moor House/Morton
6. Thornfield/Ferndean

The bullet-pointed summaries below track the stages of her journey, while the commentaries identify Charlotte Brontë's methods.

Gateshead Hall (Chapters 1–4)

Summary

- Jane, a ten-year-old orphan, lives with her aunt, Mrs Reed, at Gateshead Hall.
- The Reed children are spoilt and resentful of Jane. The eldest, John, torments her unceasingly.
- When Jane retaliates against his physical bullying, she is shut in the frightening red room in darkness.
- Terrified, she begs for release, but Mrs Reed is pitiless.
- Jane faints and the doctor suggests that she go away to school.
- The Principal of Lowood School, Mr Brocklehurst, arrives. His view of Jane is shaped by Mrs Reed's criticisms.
- Before leaving, Jane has a bitter argument with Mrs Reed.

Commentary

We see through the eyes of Jane Eyre, an orphaned girl living at Gateshead Hall. She is resented and badly treated by her aunt, Mrs Reed, and her three children. John Reed is a spoilt bully and his character (as often in the novel) is conveyed partly through his unhealthy appearance; Georgiana is vain and vacuous; Eliza is mean-minded. Jane often seeks solitary solace in the window seat, where she can read books that provide images from outside her unhappy world. When viciously attacked by John, Jane retaliates. She is banished to the red room, where her uncle had died. Terrified, she screams for release but Mrs Reed pitilessly shuts her back in. Jane falls unconscious.

The kindly local doctor, Mr Lloyd, suggests Jane go away to school. Jane meets the intimidating Principal of Lowood residential school, Mr Brocklehurst, who seems to her childish eyes 'a black pillar ... the grim face at the top ... like a carved mask' (p. 38). He believes Mrs Reed when she tells him that Jane is deceitful. Jane's independence of mind and sense of fairness are already apparent. Seething with fury and resentment, she voices her hatred towards Mrs Reed: 'People think you are a good woman, but you are bad, hard-hearted. *You* are deceitful!' (p. 44).

Key quotation

'I was a discord in Gateshead Hall; I was like nobody there; I had nothing in harmony with Mrs Reed or her children.'
(p. 19)

▲ Mrs Reed and Jane Eyre

Build critical skills

How does Charlotte Brontë use the description of his appearance to suggest the character of John Reed?

'John Reed was a schoolboy of fourteen years old; four years older than I, for I was but ten; large and stout for his age, with a dingy and unwholesome skin; thick lineaments in a spacious visage, heavy limbs and large extremities. He gorged himself habitually at table, which made him bilious, and gave him a dim and bleared eye and flabby cheeks.'
(p. 12)

Lowood School (Chapters 5–10)

Summary

- Jane arrives exhausted at Lowood School.
- She is met with kindness by the superintendent, Miss Temple.
- The school's daily regime is harsh; the food is poor and the location unhealthy.
- Jane meets Helen Burns, an older girl with whom she feels an admiring rapport.
- Mr Brocklehurst condemns Jane but Miss Temple eventually exonerates her.

- Typhoid strikes, killing many but allowing more freedom to survivors like Jane.
- Helen dies of consumption.
- As a result of the typhus outbreak, Mr Brocklehurst loses his controlling position.
- Jane makes good progress. She becomes a teacher for two years.
- When Miss Temple leaves, Jane realises her own need to move on. She accepts a post as governess at distant Thornfield Hall.

Commentary

Lowood School is based on the Clergy Daughters School at Cowan Bridge, to which Charlotte Brontë and her sisters Maria, Elizabeth and Emily were sent by their widowed father. Maria and Elizabeth died there of consumption. Jane's entry into Lowood School offers an image of her time there: an intimidating darkness that is relieved and illuminated by the kindness of Miss Temple. She is befriended by an older girl, Helen Burns, who cares more about spiritual matters than material ones. When Mr Brocklehurst visits the school he denounces Jane as a deceitful liar. She has to stand in shame on a stool for hours, 'exposed to general view on a pedestal of infamy', but Helen's smile of support helps her endure the humiliation. When Jane and Helen share a tea-and-cakes hour with Miss Temple, Jane is amazed at Helen's learning and Miss Temple's sophisticated refinement. Miss Temple investigates Mr Brocklehurst's accusations and exonerates Jane.

Key quotation

Jane declares that, 'if others don't love me, I would rather die than live – I cannot bear to be solitary and hated.' Helen replies, 'Hush, Jane! You think too much of the love of human beings; you are too impulsive, too vehement.'
(p. 82)

In Lowood School the attitudes, routines, food and even clothing are intended to break the spirit. The food is sometimes inedible: one day 'Breakfast was over, and none had breakfasted' (p. 55). When Mr Brocklehurst challenges Miss Temple over issuing extra food, Charlotte Brontë signals the contrast between them. Mr Brocklehurst's hypocrisy is shown in his harsh treatment of the girls and his indulgent attitude to his daughters. Helen Burns is victimised by Miss Scatcherd, but her calm endurance of suffering – 'Life appears to me too short to be spent in nursing animosity, or registering wrongs' (p. 69) – contrasts with Jane's outspoken indignation. Helen is ill with consumption but she is deeply religious and does not fear death. Spring brings hope, but also disease because Lowood (the name is not accidental) is low, damp and unhealthy. Typhus breaks out, but Jane is not infected and has unaccustomed freedom. Hearing that Helen is dying, Jane says, 'I must give her one last kiss, exchange with her one last word' (p. 95). Helen dies with Jane's arms around her. Jane loves and admires Helen but does not share her belief that the next world matters more than the present one.

The next eight years are not referred to in any detail, but Mr Brocklehurst is humiliated by having 'gentlemen of rather more enlarged and sympathising minds' (p. 99) put in charge of the school. After six years of excellent progress as a pupil, Jane becomes a teacher. When Miss Temple, her guide and companion, leaves to marry, Jane realises that 'the real world was wide' and having 'tired of the routine of eight years in one afternoon' decides, with the help of 'a kind fairy' (p. 103), that she needs a change. She advertises her services as a governess and accepts a post at Thornfield Hall. Before leaving Jane is visited by Bessie, the Gateshead Hall nursemaid, who thinks Jane 'quite a lady'. By contrast, the Reed children all cause problems. Bessie mentions (conveniently for the plot!) that Mr Eyre, Jane's uncle, has called, hoping to see her before leaving for Madeira.

Build critical skills

How does Charlotte Brontë use the episode of the burnt porridge (p. 55) to bring out the contrast between Mr Brocklehurst and Miss Temple?

Thornfield Hall (Chapters 11–15)

Summary

- Jane arrives at Millcote and is taken to Thornfield Hall.
- She is welcomed by Mrs Fairfax, the housekeeper, and meets her pupil, Adèle Varens, who is the ward of the Hall's owner, Mr Rochester. Jane hears strange sounds and is told that they come from a servant, Grace Poole.
- Jane becomes dissatisfied with the comfortable confines of Thornfield. One evening she helps a rider who has fallen from his horse; the horseman turns out to be her employer, Mr Rochester.
- When interrogated by Mr Rochester, Jane answers honestly and robustly, unafraid of his gruff exterior.
- Finding Jane's innocent sincerity appealing, he reveals some of his past folly, including his liaison with Adèle's mother.
- One night Jane hears sounds and unreal 'goblin laughter' outside her bedroom door. She discovers Mr Rochester's bed curtains in flames and Mr Rochester deeply asleep. She puts out the fire.
- The fire is blamed on Grace Poole.
- In the morning, Mr Rochester has gone.

Commentary

Jane thinks Mrs Fairfax might own Thornfield Hall, showing how naïve she is. Jane's pupil, eight-year-old Adèle, has extravagant French style, and her operatic song hints at a background of inappropriate, possibly sexual, behaviour. Mrs Fairfax's descriptions of Mr Rochester intrigue rather than inform. Increasingly restless, Jane yearns for the wider world that she encounters only in her imagination.

Charlotte Brontë offers us an image of the later relationship between Jane and Mr Rochester in their very first meeting. The atmosphere is one of moonlight and myth: she is thinking of a spirit creature called a Gytrash when a large dog appears. Next comes a horse and rider, but the horse slips

Key quotation

'It is in vain to say human beings ought to be satisfied with tranquillity: they must have action; and they will make it if they cannot find it.'
(p. 129)

Build critical skills

Which are the key words Charlotte Brontë uses to create the magical atmosphere surrounding the first meeting of Jane and Mr Rochester?

Key quotation

Mr Rochester claims he 'was thrust on to a wrong tack, at the age of one-and-twenty' and 'since happiness is irrevocably denied me, I have a right to get pleasure out of life.' (p. 160)

on ice and the rider falls. Since he seems neither heroic nor so handsome that she is disconcerted, she calmly offers help. He remounts with Jane's aid, leaning on her shoulder. Unaware of his identity, Jane returns to Thornfield to find that Mr Rochester has arrived, but that he had a fall on the way.

Jane finds Mr Rochester gruff but not intimidating. He claims that he thought her a fairy (a favourite term of his for her) who had bewitched his horse, but notes improvement in Adèle. When Mr Rochester questions Jane she is honest and factual. When she admits she does not find him handsome, Mr Rochester comments, 'not three in three thousand raw schoolgirl-governesses would have answered me as you have just done' (p. 158). Mr Rochester's conversation is so untypical of a master/employer discussion that Jane says, 'though I am bewildered I am certainly not afraid.' Mrs Fairfax mentions that Mr Rochester had 'family troubles' some years ago, which help to explain his frequent absences.

The reader notes the growing sexual attraction between Jane and Mr Rochester. He recounts his liaison with Adèle's mother, Céline Varens, a French opera dancer, and how that relationship ended. Jane reflects on the change in Mr Rochester's attitude towards her – 'I never seemed in his way' – and feels 'as if he were my relation rather than my master' (p. 171). That night, Jane hears a murmuring sound and a 'demoniac laugh'. Courageously she investigates, finding Mr Rochester's bed curtains aflame and him deeply asleep. She soaks him and the bedclothes, thereby putting out the fire and saving his life. Mr Rochester's gratitude is evident. 'You have saved my life: I have a pleasure in owing you so immense a debt' (p. 176). Jane is unable to sleep, 'tossed on a buoyant but unquiet sea' of emotions, since she has finally registered Mr Rochester's feelings towards her.

Build critical skills

As readers will note, Mr Rochester is reluctant to release Jane's hand after she has saved his life. How does Charlotte Brontë present the growing affection between them?

▲ Jane discovers the fire in Rochester's bedroom (1970 TV film adaptation)

Thornfield Hall (Chapters 16–20)

Summary

- Mr Rochester leaves Thornfield without a word.
- Jane learns he intends to return with a large party, including beautiful Miss Blanche Ingram.
- Jane tells herself that she has imagined that Mr Rochester feels affection for her.
- The guests arrive and Jane's presence is commanded. She is increasingly distressed at the thought that Mr Rochester could marry Blanche.
- While Mr Rochester is away Mr Mason, a previous acquaintance, arrives.
- An old beggarwoman tells people's fortunes but Jane realises that 'she' is Mr Rochester.
- On hearing that Mason has arrived Mr Rochester is visibly shaken.
- That night Jane is woken by a fearful shriek. Mason is bleeding from an attack. She stays with him while Mr Rochester fetches a surgeon.
- Next morning Mr Rochester and Jane talk in the garden, but much is left unspoken.

Commentary

The morning after the fire leaves Jane enjoined to silence and puzzled that Mr Rochester has left. Grace Poole (assumed by Jane to be the culprit) acts as if nothing had happened. When she hears of Blanche Ingram, a lady who could be Mr Rochester's future bride, Jane's hopes are dashed. To control what she now sees as romantic fantasies, she disciplines herself to draw a self-portrait, emphasising her own plainness, and to create a contrasting picture of accomplished, beautiful Blanche. Jane observes the guests while trying to remain unobserved. The others are crisply described and dismissed but Blanche is 'moulded like a Diana', talented at the piano and clearly admired by all, including Mr Rochester. Jane has eyes only for him and now acknowledges her own feelings.

Key quotation

'He made me love him without looking at me. ... I know I must conceal my sentiments: I must smother hope; I must remember that he cannot care much for me.'
(pp. 203–4)

▲ Rochester with Blanche Ingram in the 2011 film adaptation

Blanche's comments on governesses ('half of them are detestable and the rest ridiculous...') show that Charlotte Brontë is deliberately setting her up as Jane's opposite. The superficial gaiety of Mr Rochester's flirting with Blanche contrasts with the unspoken depth of emotion in his relationship with Jane. Jane, perceiving Blanche's shallow cruelty and coldness, is horrified that Rochester seems bent on marrying Blanche 'because her rank and connexions suited him'. Jane claims to the reader that she is not jealous and does not blame Mr Rochester for marrying without love, since she assumes that, 'All their class held these principles'.

The guests, especially Blanche, do not find the fortune-telling comforting. Jane, however, gives as good as she gets verbally and finds the old gypsy woman's curious questions 'a web of mystification' until 'she' is finally revealed as Mr Rochester. When she tells him that Mason has arrived, he is startled and concerned. Later, the household is awoken by a shrill, sharp cry. Other guests, nearly hysterical, are told of a servant's nightmare, but Jane calmly and courageously accompanies Mr Rochester to where Mason lies bathed in blood. She stays with him, aware of a snarling noise in a nearby room, until Rochester returns with a surgeon. This 'Gothic' episode has a strangely eerie atmosphere, with 'darkening shadows' and 'flickering gleams'. Jane wonders what mystery 'lurks in the house.' First-time readers, too, wonder about this 'web of horror'.

Build critical skills

The episode of the old gypsy woman strains a reader's credulity. Why do you think Charlotte Brontë included it?

Gateshead Hall revisited (Chapter 21)

Summary

- Jane learns of John Reed's death and that Mrs Reed has asked for her.
- She returns to Gateshead Hall.
- Mrs Reed admits to having felt jealous of Jane and that Jane's uncle, John Eyre, had written to say that he wished Jane to inherit his fortune, but that the letter had not been sent on.
- Mrs Reed dies without having been reconciled with Jane.
- The Reed sisters, Eliza and Georgiana, hate each other and neither is much distressed by the death of their brother or their mother.

Commentary

This chapter shows us that Jane has developed, while the Reed sisters have grown rather than changed: Georgiana lives for society; Eliza seeks only to avoid it. Jane forgives Mrs Reed but the forgiveness is not mutual. Mrs Reed confesses to having broken her promise to her dying husband to look after Jane as her own, and to having told Jane's uncle that Jane had died at Lowood. Evidence of Jane's emotional maturity is shown in that she stays some weeks at Gateshead Hall before returning to Thornfield and reflects, 'Eliza did not mortify me, nor Georgiana ruffle me.'

Back at Thornfield (Chapters 22–27)

Summary

- Jane is warmly welcomed back to Thornfield.
- Mr Rochester teases Jane about marrying Blanche, before declaring his love for her.
- Once Jane believes him to be serious, she accepts him.
- Prior to their wedding, Jane deliberately keeps Mr Rochester at a distance.
- Two nights before the wedding, Jane has disturbing dreams and her bedroom is visited by a nightmare figure who leaves real traces. Mr Rochester, visibly shaken, blames Grace Poole.
- The marriage ceremony is interrupted because Mr Rochester 'has a wife now living'. This is affirmed by Richard Mason.
- Rochester confirms the charge and takes everyone to see his mad wife.
- Jane learns that it was her letter to her uncle in Madeira that brought about Mason's intervention.
- Rochester tells Jane the whole of his story and re-affirms his love for her, but she is determined not to be his mistress.
- She leaves Thornfield during the night.

Build critical skills

Why do you think Charlotte Brontë uses dialogue such as the extract below to reveal the attitudes of Eliza and Georgiana, rather than describing them in Jane's words?

Eliza: '"I can tell you this — if the whole human race, ourselves excepted, were swept away, and we two stood alone on the earth, I would leave you in the old world, and betake myself to the new."

She closed her lips.

"You might have spared yourself the trouble of delivering that tirade," answered Georgiana. "Everybody knows you are the most selfish, heartless creature in existence: and I know your spiteful hatred towards me."'

(p. 272)

Commentary

Build critical skills

Why do you think Charlotte Brontë made Mr Rochester so cruel to Jane before asking her to marry him?

The pleasant weather on Jane's return to Thornfield is again an indicator of mood and now there is no doubt about her feelings for Mr Rochester – 'never had I loved him so well.' Jane tells him that 'wherever you are is my home – my only home' (p. 283).

Mr Rochester teases Jane, emphasising her servant status and suggesting that he will be marrying Miss Ingram. He (cruelly) goes as far as saying, 'Adèle must go to school; and you, Miss Eyre, must get a new situation' (p. 289). He even mentions a post in Ireland at Bitternutt Lodge with Mrs O'Gall. (Note the names!)

In a different tone he then says, 'it is as if I had a string somewhere under my left ribs, tightly and inextricably knotted to a similar string situated in the corresponding quarter of your little frame' (p. 291). Jane is unable to control her feelings any longer.

> 'Do you think, because I am poor, obscure, plain, and little, I am soulless and heartless? ... I have as much soul as you – and full as much heart! ... it is my spirit that addresses your spirit; just as if both had passed through the grave, and we stood at God's feet, equal – as we are!'
>
> (p. 292)

She resists his embrace with the words 'I am a free human being with an independent will, which I now exert to leave you.' When he says, 'I offer you my heart, my hand, and a share of all my possessions', Jane is disbelieving until she begins 'in his earnestness – and especially his incivility – to credit his sincerity' (p. 294). Finally she accepts him by his name, Edward. Jane does not react when he cries, 'God pardon me! ... and man meddle not with me: I have her and will hold her' (p. 295). For readers, however, that strikes a strange note, amplified by the change in the weather. The wind is roaring and the chestnut tree beneath which they sit 'writhed and groaned'. Lightning flashes and rain rushes down as they head for shelter – a signal that makes a reader sense that the path of this love will not be smooth. A bemused Mrs Fairfax witnesses their goodnight kiss. A symbol for the reader to remember is that the great horse-chestnut tree has been struck by lightning and split in half.

Build critical skills

Charlotte Brontë often links the weather with events in her characters' lives and destinies. How does she signal to a reader that the intended marriage of Jane and Mr Rochester is likely to meet difficulties?

Jane wonders if what has happened was a dream, but looks at her face in a mirror and 'felt that it was no longer plain.' She can hardly comprehend when Rochester calls her 'Jane Rochester' and is uncomfortable with his plans to dress her finely; she begs him 'not to send for the jewels and don't crown me with roses.' Rochester claims, not wholly convincingly for the reader, that he feigned courtship of Miss Ingram to make Jane jealous. Charlotte Brontë plants a significant exchange that readers will remember later:

> Jane: '"You have a curious, designing mind, Mr. Rochester, I am afraid your principles on some points are eccentric."
>
> "My principles were never trained, Jane."'
>
> (p. 303)

Mrs Fairfax is disconcerted by the news since it is her view that 'Gentlemen in his station are not accustomed to marry their governesses' (p. 306).

Shopping for dresses and jewels makes Jane feel like a 'doll'. She writes to her Uncle John in the hope that she might have the prospect of some fortune one day. Determined to keep Rochester at a distance until they are married, she remains 'flinty' to cool his ardour, yet admits, 'often I would rather have pleased than teased him' (p. 316). Jane's independence of spirit endures despite her feeling that, 'My future husband was becoming to me my whole world; and more than the world: almost my hope of heaven' (p. 316).

All is ready for the wedding but Jane cannot bring herself to put on the luggage labels for a Mrs Rochester. She has 'trouble of mind', which develops into 'hypochondriac foreboding' since she had disturbing dreams the night before, the weather is ominously blustery and the moon is 'blood-red and half-overcast'. Jane's sense of foreboding is tangible: 'everything in life seems unreal' and 'I wish this present hour would never end: who knows with what fate the next may come charged?' (p. 322). She recounts her dreams of a young child, then of ruined Thornfield and waking with a vampire-like woman in her room. This figure wore and then tore her new veil. Mr Rochester claims that Jane imagined the figure but she knows that 'the thing was real' and her evidence is the ripped veil.

When the wedding is halted by Mason and the lawyer on the grounds of an existing marriage, Rochester decides 'all shall bolt out at once, like a bullet from the barrel'. He takes them to see his wife, Bertha, who is 'like some strange wild animal' (p. 338). Jane recognises her as the night visitant. Bertha attacks Rochester and is pinioned to a chair while Rochester compares 'this young girl, who stands so quiet and grave at the mouth of hell' with the 'demon' he is married to (p. 339).

It was Jane's letter to her uncle that had provoked Mason's intervention. She felt 'a cold, solitary girl again: her life was pale; her prospects were desolate' (p. 341). Much that was mysterious is now clear. Like Jane, the first-time reader reviews whether Rochester's conduct can be understood or justified. 'Mr. Rochester was not to me what he had been; for he was not what I had thought him' (p. 341). Sorrow overwhelms her. Jane wants to leave Thornfield, yet cannot make herself do so. Mr Rochester waits for her and she instantly forgives him.

Key quotation

'I loved him very much – more than I could trust myself to say – more than words had power to express.'
(p. 304)

▲ Bertha tearing the veil

Key quotation

'Reader, I forgave him at the moment and on the spot. ... I forgave him all: yet not in words, not outwardly; only at my heart's core.'
(p. 344)

Seeing his passion for her undimmed, Jane admits to herself, 'I *do* love you ... more than ever: but I must not show or indulge the feeling; and this is the last time I must express it' (p. 350). She declares that she must leave Thornfield and Rochester, uttering a cry of 'God help me!' as she sees his suffering. He, however, envisages her accompanying him to live in the south of France. Rochester tells how his father tricked him into marrying Bertha Mason, not unwillingly, given her supposed fortune, his passionate nature and since she was 'tall, dark and majestic'. He admits 'I was dazzled, stimulated: my senses were excited; and being ignorant, raw and inexperienced, I thought I loved her' (p. 352). Her shallow coarseness, vicious temper and growing insanity meant that he rapidly developed a deep antipathy towards her. He brought her to Thornfield and fled to Europe to distract himself.

Now he feels contempt for his own conduct. He sought love through a sequence of mistresses, but until Jane he had found no one he could love. He had found her 'full of strange contrasts' but 'refined by nature', although 'absolutely unused to society'. Jane is much moved as he recounts his growing and passionate love for her. She feels that 'Not a human being that ever lived could wish to be loved better than I was loved', but she 'shuddered to hear the infatuated assertion' that they could be together. After a 'terrible moment: full of struggle, blackness, burning', she declares 'Mr Rochester, I will *not* be yours' and 'Do as I do: trust in God and yourself. Believe in heaven. Hope to meet again there' (p. 364). Rochester wants her to 'transgress a mere human law' but she refuses. When asked who cares for her, Jane replies that she cares for herself. She finally, bravely, kisses him, goes to her room and, despite knowing how desperate Rochester will be, steals away before dawn.

Key quotation

Jane declares she will 'keep the law given by God; sanctioned by man.'
(p. 365)

Moor House/Morton (Chapters 28–35)

Summary

- Jane wanders, desperate and increasingly destitute, for three days.
- Ill from exhaustion, she is finally taken in to a house with two sisters and their brother, St John Rivers.
- Jane is recognised as a cultivated lady and befriended by the sisters, Diana and Mary.
- St John Rivers offers her a teaching post at a new girls' school.
- The Rivers family's Uncle John dies, but without leaving them the legacy they had hoped for.
- Jane starts teaching in the local school and meets Rosamond Oliver, a local heiress who is in love with St John Rivers. He puts his mission before his love.

- St John Rivers reveals Jane as their cousin and an heiress. Overjoyed to have a family, Jane wants the inheritance to be shared between them.
- Jane tries to please St John and even starts learning Hindustani, but is increasingly stifled by St John's influence.
- St John asks Jane to accompany him to India. She agrees to this, but not to his demand for marriage.
- Jane senses Rochester crying out her name and wants only to return to Thornfield.

Commentary

Jane pays a heavy price for her strength of mind and we share her suffering. For three days she wanders in the wilderness of the countryside, hungry, exhausted and reduced to begging. She feels cut off from human society and ready to die. At last she sees a light in the darkness of night and through the window sees two graceful young women who 'were all delicacy and cultivation'. Jane feels she has much in common with them (later proving justified), but their servant Hannah sends her away. The master of the house, a clergyman called St John Rivers, finds her desperate on the doorstep and takes her in. The sisters Diana and Mary are intrigued by Jane, and she even wins over Hannah. Jane gratefully tells the family her story, but claims that her name is Jane Elliott and that 'not a tie links me to any living thing'.

Physically St John is conventionally appealing, but in a way that contrasts with Mr Rochester. He is 'young' – aged 28–30 years old, with blue eyes and fair hair. St John has 'a reserved, an abstracted and even ... a brooding nature' (p. 404), very different from the warmth and generosity of his sisters. He appears to believe, accept and respect Jane for her honesty and readiness to work.

St John Rivers is a powerful preacher. When he offers her the post of teacher (which he regards as trivial and 'cramping') at the new girls' school, Jane accepts without hesitation.

Build critical skills

In the passage below, how does Charlotte Brontë use words about coldness to suggest the character of St John Rivers?

'Besides, I was out of practice in talking to him: his reserve was again frozen over, and my frankness was congealed beneath it. He had not kept his promise of treating me like his sisters; he continually made little chilling differences between us, which did not at all tend to the development of cordiality: in short, now that I was acknowledged his kinswoman, and lived under the same roof with him, I felt the distance between us to be far greater than when he had known me only as the village school-mistress. When I remembered how far I had once been admitted to his confidence, I could hardly comprehend his present frigidity.'
(p. 456)

News arrives that an uncle of the Rivers family has died, but has left his fortune to another relative rather than to them. The family accepts this philosophically. Diana and Mary return to their governess posts and Jane starts teaching. Jane is grateful for her new home – a cottage – and for her role as teacher, but although not regretting her decision, she 'felt desolate to a degree.' St John counsels her 'to resist firmly every temptation which would incline you to look back' (p. 416). Jane meets Rosamond Oliver and damns her with faint praise as 'sufficiently intelligent' and 'coquettish, but not heartless ... She had been indulged from her birth, but was not absolutely spoilt' (p. 425). Jane nevertheless encourages St John to marry her, but while acknowledging he is 'acutely sensible to her charms', he cannot see Rosamond as a missionary's wife.

Key quotation

St John Rivers comments to Jane that: 'human affections and sympathies have a most powerful hold on you.'
(p. 409)

St John realises that Jane is 'original' and 'not timid.' He admits that 'Reason, and not feeling, is my guide: my ambition is unlimited' (p. 432). Mysteriously, he tears off a strip of Jane's drawing paper. When St John returns next day, struggling through a snowstorm, he brings the news that Jane is an heiress worth £20,000 and that she and the Rivers family are cousins. Jane's initial reaction is to value finding relations more than the fortune. Her second is characteristically generous and, 'contrary to all custom', she wants the money to be shared between the four of them.

Key quotation

St John tells Jane that she is 'formed for labour, not for love. A missionary's wife you must – shall be. You shall be mine.'
(p. 464)

Astonishingly, St John Rivers claims Jane 'not for my pleasure, but for my Sovereign's service', but she feels 'an iron shroud contracted round me', feeling that she abandons half of herself if she goes to India to a premature death. 'He prizes me as a soldier would a good weapon, and that is all' (p. 467). St John demands marriage but Jane offers him 'only a comrade's constancy', scorning his idea of love. Jane finds it hard to endure his 'iron silence' and the permanence of his disapproval. She says, 'If I were to marry you, you would kill me. You are killing me now.' St John responds with controlled fury but Jane repeats her refusal to marry him, and will not go to India just to please him. She wants to know what has happened to Mr Rochester, a concern that St John sees as 'lawless and unconsecrated'. She tells Diana, 'He is a good and a great man; but he forgets, pitilessly, the feelings and claims of little people in pursuing his own large views' (p. 479).

Build critical skills

Why does Charlotte Brontë have Jane hearing a cry from Rochester that mysteriously comes from far beyond hearing distance? Which other happenings in the novel are difficult to explain in 'ordinary' terms?

When St John renews his pressure on Jane to change her mind, she is on the point of weakening when suddenly, almost magically, an 'inexpressible feeling' thrills through her heart as she hears Rochester's voice calling her name. This breaks St John's spell over her for good.

Ferndean (Chapters 36–38)

Summary

- Jane returns to Thornfield and finds it a charred ruin.
- She hears how Bertha started a fire, in which she died and Mr Rochester was blinded and maimed.
- Jane seeks out Mr Rochester at Ferndean.
- He is encouraged by her words to propose to her again.
- They marry rapidly and live lovingly together.

Commentary

The voice Jane had heard 'seemed in me – not in the external world.' She journeys back to find Thornfield 'a blackened ruin' with 'the silence of death about it'. Jane learns that Rochester had been desperate to find her, and that Bertha had started the fire that gutted Thornfield and had jumped to her death from the battlements. Rochester was left 'stone-blind' and maimed when the house collapsed on him because he would not leave until all were safe.

Jane learns that Rochester now lives at Ferndean Manor, 'blind and a cripple'. She hastens there and sees Rochester 'a caged eagle' in his helplessness. At first he cannot believe that the voice is hers. Her embrace convinces him but he fears that she cannot care for 'a sightless block' such as himself. She starts to 'rehumanise' him. To his amazement when she sees the stump of his arm she says 'one is in danger of loving you too well for all this' (p. 503). Jane feels that 'in his presence I thoroughly lived; and he lived in mine.' When Rochester asks, 'Am I hideous, Jane?' her reply is typically poised – 'Very, Sir; you always were you know.' To herself she admits that 'the powerlessness of the strong man touched my heart to the quick.' Jane uses Rochester's jealousy of the 'graceful Apollo' St John to combat his sadness, but admits that St John was 'as cold as an iceberg' and that she did not love him.

Although 'an irreligious dog', Rochester acknowledges his gratitude to God, 'who sees not as man sees, and judges not as man judges.' He admits that he did wrong and has been justly punished. He experiences 'remorse, repentance: the wish for reconcilement to my Maker' (p. 514). It emerges that he cried out to Jane at the very moment she heard a cry, and that he heard her response that 'I am coming.' This is a coincidence that Jane thinks 'too awful and inexplicable to be communicated or discussed.' We see again the image, first seen when his horse slipped, of Rochester with his hand on Jane, who 'served both for his prop and his guide.'

Key quotation

When Rochester asks Jane to marry him, she accepts because 'to be your wife is, for me, to be as happy as I can be on earth.' She declares that 'I love you better now, when I can really be useful to you, than I did in your state of proud independence.'
(p. 513)

'Reader, I married him' (p. 517). And so she did, within three days, in a quiet wedding. Adèle is rescued from school, and Diana and Mary are both happily married. Mr Rochester recovers some of his sight, while St John lives and dies for his ambition in India.

Significantly, the final words of the novel are St John's – 'Amen; even so, come, Lord Jesus.'

Structure

Each stage in Jane's progress features significant challenges, through which her sense of self develops and is shared with the reader. For example, when Jane leaves Lowood, Charlotte Brontë (in older Jane's voice) announces this as a new phase in Jane's life. 'A new chapter in a novel is something like a new scene in a play; and when I draw up the curtain this time, reader, you must fancy you see a room in the George Inn at Millcote' (p. 111). Jane shares her thoughts more directly with the reader from that point on and this culminates, famously, in 'Reader, I married him' (p. 517).

GRADE BOOSTER

Usually an examination question will explain briefly where in the novel the extract is taken from. It won't necessarily tell you what happens just before or just after the extract. You don't *need* to know this, but when writing about plot and structure, it can be helpful to know. For example, you may be able to refer to the use of contrast with other events, **foreshadowing** or dramatic irony. So make sure you have a really clear grasp of the order of events.

Foreshadowing: a technique used to warn the reader of a future event.

The stages of Jane's development vary in duration and in the proportion of the novel that is devoted to them. Her last eight years at Lowood take a few lines, while the months at Thornfield, the emotional core of the story, take up nearly half of the novel. The timeline of the novel is shown on the opposite page.

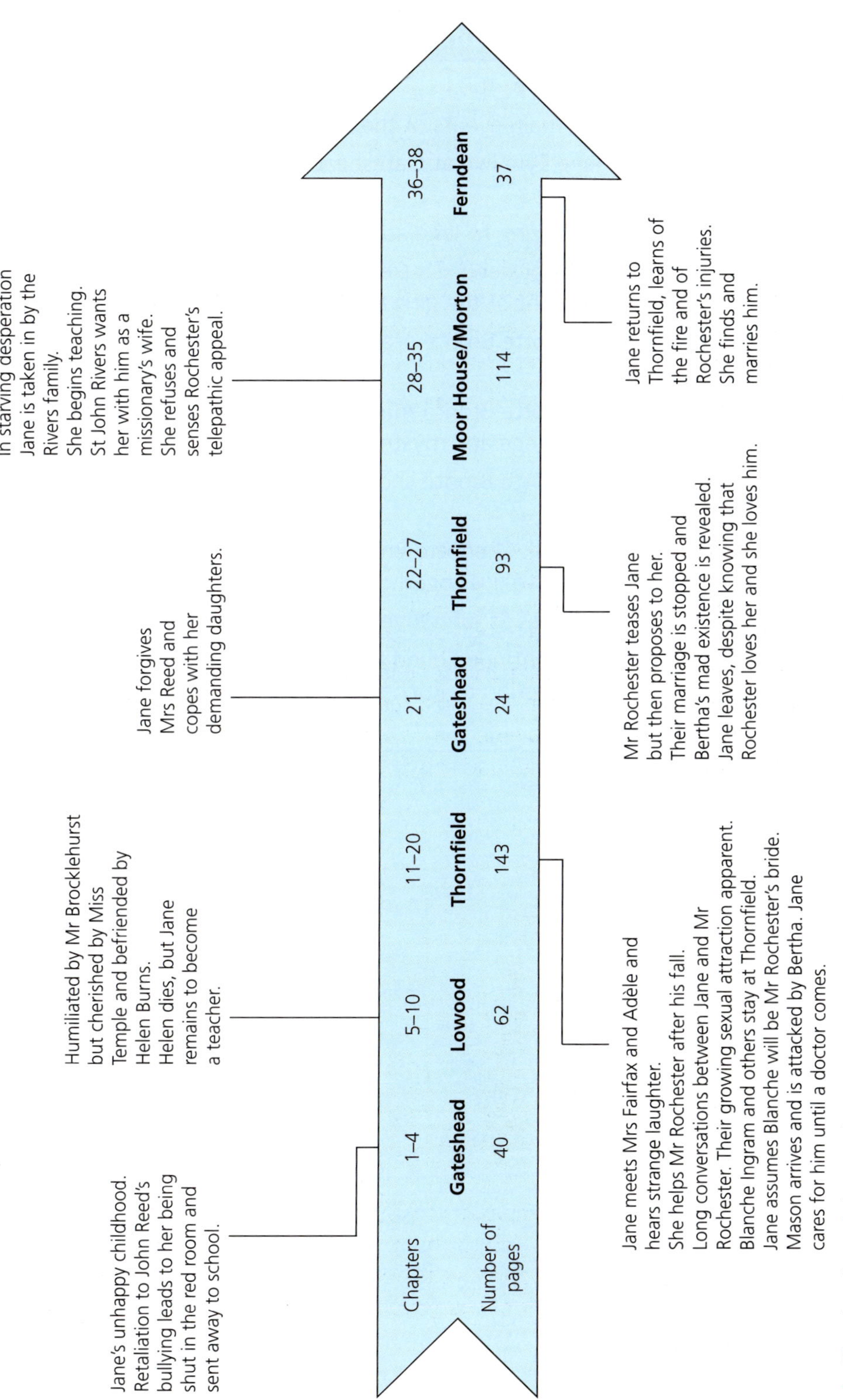

▲ The timeline of the novel

GRADE FOCUS

Grade 5

To achieve a Grade 5, students must show a clear and detailed understanding of the whole text and the effects created by its structure.

Grade 8

To achieve a Grade 8, students' responses will display a comprehensive understanding of implicit and explicit meanings in the text as a whole and will examine and evaluate in detail the writer's use of structure.

REVIEW YOUR LEARNING

(Answers are given on p. 108.)

1. Where do the main events of the novel take place?
2. Why does Jane Eyre live at Gateshead Hall if the family resent her?
3. What is so terrifying to Jane about being shut in the red room?
4. How does Mr Brocklehurst's treatment of his daughters compare with his treatment of the girls at Lowood?
5. How does Charlotte Brontë prepare the reader for news of Jane's inheritance?
6. How does Charlotte Brontë make Mr Rochester's first meeting with Jane so strange and mysterious?
7. How does Charlotte Brontë show the shallowness of the guests at Thornfield?
8. Why do you think Charlotte Brontë had Jane refuse Mr Rochester's plan to live together unmarried?
9. In what ways does St John Rivers contrast with Mr Rochester?
10. 'Mr Rochester continued blind the first two years of our union.' What is your reaction to Rochester's remarkable recovery of sight?

Characterisation

Target your thinking

- Who are the key characters in the novel? (**AO1**)
- How does Charlotte Brontë present the main characters? (**AO2**)
- How do the characters compare with each other? (**AO1**, **AO2**)
- What do they each contribute to the novel? (**AO1**, **AO2**, **AO3**)

Charlotte Brontë uses a variety of techniques to present each of the characters in *Jane Eyre* to the readers:

- The description of the character, including appearance, body language and setting.
- The life circumstances and actions of the character.
- What the character says.
- What other characters say about them.
- The comments of the narrator about the character.
- The development (or otherwise) of the character.
- How the characters contrast with each other.

GRADE BOOSTER

Remember that the characters in the novel have been created by a writer. Focus on how the writer makes the characters come alive for the reader. Don't write about the characters as if they were real people. If the words 'Charlotte Brontë' or 'the writer' don't appear several times in your answer, you are probably not answering the question and so you are unlikely to achieve high marks. When you write about characters, mention that they are the author's creation, e.g. write 'Charlotte Brontë makes Jane a deliberate contrast with Blanche Ingram', rather than just writing 'Jane is very different from Blanche Ingram.'

Characters in the novel

Jane Eyre

Charlotte Brontë presents Jane Eyre as the reader's companion and confidante throughout the novel. Beneath Jane's quietly demure exterior is a strong, principled and passionate woman. She is not an 'imp', 'elf'

Key quotation

Jane: 'Do you think, because I am poor, obscure, plain, and little, I am soulless and heartless?'
(p. 292)

Key quotation

Jane declares at Lowood that 'if others don't love me, I would rather die than live – I cannot bear to be solitary and hated'
(p. 82)

or 'fairy' (Rochester's frequent terms for her), she is herself, and she consistently refuses to allow others to define her: at Gateshead Hall she rejects the role of the dependent relation who can be bullied and mistreated: '*Speak* I must: I had been trodden on severely, and *must* turn' (p. 43). As this quotation shows, Charlotte Brontë has deliberately depicted Jane as unlike Helen Burns: Jane fights for what she thinks is right in *this* world rather than the next, and although some characters condemn her passionate responses (e.g. Mrs Reed says, '...you are passionate Jane, that you must allow'), most readers admire her spirit. Jane is shown to be honest with herself and others ('I should not like to belong to poor people', p. 30).

Charlotte Brontë has Jane facing different challenges at the different stages of her development. For example, on leaving Lowood she has to cope with life unaided for the first time and confides to the reader, 'It is a very strange sensation to inexperienced youth to feel itself quite alone in the world, cut adrift from every connection' (p. 111). As an orphan Jane has a deep need to belong, to be wanted and to be loved.

She delights in discovering that the Rivers family are her family. St John Rivers correctly observes that 'human affections and sympathies have a most powerful hold on you' (p. 409), while Rochester says, 'I saw you had a social heart' (p. 362).

Build critical skills

'I was left there alone – winner of the field. It was the hardest battle I had fought, and the first victory I had gained. I stood awhile on the rug, where Mr Brocklehurst had stood, and I enjoyed my conqueror's solitude. First, I smiled to myself and felt elate; but this fierce pleasure subsided in me as fast as did the accelerated throb of my pulses. A child cannot quarrel with its elders, as I had done – cannot give its furious feelings uncontrolled play, as I had given mine – without experiencing afterwards the pang of remorse and the chill of reaction.'
(p. 45)

How has Charlotte Brontë used the voice of the narrator to make this description of the aftermath of Jane's quarrel with Mrs Reed effective for the reader?

The challenges she faces often focus on feelings. It is one type of challenge to win the respect, then the love, of Mr Rochester, but it is a very different one to resist her own passion and his desire to take her away as his mistress to the south of France because she feels that it would be wrong in God's eyes. It is different again to resist the pressures of duty and to refuse to marry St John Rivers, even when it seemed that 'Religion called – Angels beckoned – God commanded' (p. 482). Jane has the self-knowledge to admit, 'I know no medium: I never in my life have known any medium in my dealings with positive, hard characters, antagonistic to my own, between absolute submission and determined revolt' (p. 462). She declares that, 'I want to enjoy my own faculties as well as to cultivate those of other people' (p. 450) and Charlotte Brontë gives her the words, 'It was *my* time to assume ascendancy. *My* powers were in play and in force' (p. 484).

One thing not in Jane's power is her appearance, yet she is very conscious of it and it is referred to throughout the novel. The author draws early attention to the way judgements are made based on appearance and Jane winces inwardly when Bessie comments that 'you were no beauty as a child', since 'At eighteen most people wish to please, and the conviction that they have not an exterior likely to second that desire brings anything but gratification' (p. 108). It takes her a long time to believe that Mr Rochester could love someone as unprepossessing as herself. Her drawings of herself and Blanche Ingram are done to keep her romantic fantasies in place. After Mr Rochester has asked for her hand, 'I looked at my face in the glass, and felt it was no longer plain' (p. 297). She resists being dressed up like a 'doll' before her wedding since that would not be true to her nature.

Although aware of the (lack of) impact of her own appearance, Jane herself does not judge on appearances – she rejects St John, who looks like a 'graceful Apollo', and instead accepts Rochester, despite his being 'a Vulcan – a real blacksmith, brown, broad-shouldered; and blind and lame into the bargain' (p. 509).

Another arena of challenge for Jane is the social one, where, often, appearance is all. Charlotte Brontë was unhappy as a governess, so there is real meaning in the social progress made by a mere orphan-turned-governess who marries into an aristocratic family. Jane is shown observing the social charades rather than participating in them. The people she values (like Bessie, Mary and Diane, or Mrs Fairfax) tend to be those without money and pretensions. By contrast, Blanche Ingram and the guests at Thornfield are deemed not worthy of Jane's serious regard. Jane is not jealous of Blanche since she is 'too inferior to excite the feeling.'

The author shows Jane as physically courageous on a number of occasions, such as when she helps Mr Rochester after his fall, saves him from fire, or tends to Mason when he is bleeding and his attacker is still audible. As Rochester later observes, 'Never was anything at once so frail and so indomitable' (p. 366). She is also spiritually strong: although not focused on God's love in the way that Helen Burns is, she tries always to act in a moral, broadly Christian, way. She will not transgress what she sees as divine law by giving in to Rochester's immoral proposal, but she is full of forgiveness for him.

Key quotation

'I will keep the law given by God; sanctioned by man.'
(p. 365)

Key quotation

Rochester to Jane: 'You – poor and obscure, and small and plain as you are – I entreat to accept me as a husband.'
(p. 294)

Build critical skills

Jane always wishes 'to please as much as my want of beauty would permit'. How does this comment, given to Jane by the author, add to a reader's view of her character?

Key quotation

When wounded Rochester asks 'Am I hideous, Jane?' her reply is – 'Very, sir; you always were, you know.'
(p. 505)

Build critical skills

'My Edward and I, then, are happy: and the more so, because those we most love are happy likewise.' (p. 520)

How convincing is Jane as a character and as a narrator in the final chapter?

Mr Rochester questions Jane on whether she is 'altogether a human being'; she answers that she believes so and, despite her 'fairy-like' ability to sense that which cannot be seen, most readers would agree.

Edward Fairfax Rochester

Our reactions to Rochester as a character are influenced by Charlotte Brontë's technique of showing him to us only through Jane's eyes: we hear his words but we never hear his thoughts, only her thoughts about him. The author creates Rochester in the tradition of 'Gothic' heroes: as an intriguing character rather than an admirable one. He is portrayed as a passionate, powerful man, intelligent and capable of great sensitivity, but moody and deeply marred by his earlier experience of marriage to a woman who became mad. His conduct makes him problematic for first-time readers, who might sympathise with his plight once they know he is shackled to a madwoman, but who cannot ignore his playing with Jane's emotions over Blanche Ingram, nor his readiness to trick or persuade her into the role of his mistress.

Build critical skills

How might readers in the 1840s have reacted to Rochester's declaration that 'I meant ... to be a bigamist; but fate has out-manoeuvred me' (p. 336)? Would modern readers think differently?

Even before the fire at Thornfield he is not handsome, as Jane tells him. Her first observations of him are that he was 'past youth, but had not reached middle age', with 'a dark face, with stern features and a heavy brow; his eyes and gathered eyebrows looked ireful and thwarted' (p. 134). It is only his frown and his roughness that make her feel at ease in helping him. He has a masculine appeal, a powerful presence and a depth of passion that she finds irresistible. Once she comes to know him, his appearance matters less to her than his uncanny ability to tell what she is feeling.

Build critical skills

How does Charlotte Brontë use imagery here to suggest to the reader that Rochester's passion is almost irresistible?

'He seemed to devour me with his flaming glance: physically, I felt, at the moment, powerless as stubble exposed to the draught and glow of a furnace.' (p. 365)

Key quotation

'Mr Rochester had sometimes read my unspoken thoughts with an acumen to me incomprehensible.' (p. 283)

Rochester's inner self-doubt is great, yet his outward self-confidence borders on arrogance. He is accustomed to command: Mrs Fairfax says that he 'has a gentleman's tastes and habits, and he expects to have things managed in conformity to them' (p. 124). His first appearance in the novel is significant and symbolic – he bursts into the story as powerfully as a mythical figure, but his horse slips and he injures himself in the fall. He needs Jane's help to remount. That pattern is visible again at the end of the novel, when Jane becomes the guide of a burnt and blinded Rochester.

Build critical skills

What image of Mr Rochester does Charlotte Brontë create in the reader's mind through the use of sounds and images in the passage below?

'A rude noise broke on these fine ripplings and whisperings, at once so far away and so clear: a positive tramp, tramp, a metallic clatter, which effaced the soft wave-wanderings; as, in a picture, the solid mass of a crag, or the rough boles of a great oak, drawn in dark and strong on the foreground, efface the aërial distance of azure hill, sunny horizon, and blended clouds, where tint melts into tint.'
(p. 132)

Rochester has a big heart: he will not condemn his mad wife to an unhealthy house and is wounded saving others from the fire. Mr Rochester is 'a very good master' (p. 124) but is contemptuous of social conventions, not least because he was entrapped by them into a disastrous marriage.

As his attitude to Blanche Ingram shows, he is uninfluenced by wealth or social status. This is evident in his relationship with Jane: rather than maintaining conventional class boundaries, Rochester makes her feel 'as if he were my relation rather than my master.' He is never more appealing to modern readers than when he exclaims, 'Station! station! – your station is in my heart, and on the necks of those who would insult you, now or hereafter' (p. 304).

Rochester feels that he lives a life on the volcano edge – 'To live, for me, Jane, is to stand on a crater-crust which may crack and spue fire any day' (p. 250). He has tried dissipation as a way of distracting himself from himself, but he knows how dissatisfying that has proved. 'I approached the verge of despair' (p. 354) thinking 'This life ... is hell' (p. 355). Once he finds Jane, and sees her as his salvation, he is always conscious that destiny, like one of the hags in *Macbeth*, seeks to destroy his chance of happiness. Despite that, he is courageous enough to try to defeat his destiny – 'I have a right to get pleasure out of life: and I *will* get it, cost what it may' (p. 160).

Key quotation

Rochester: 'this is what I wished to have ... this young girl, who stands so grave and quiet at the mouth of hell, looking collectedly at the gambols of a demon.'
(p. 339)

Initially Rochester seems selfishly ready to ask Jane to pay some of the cost of his acquiring happiness, but he too is on a journey of development and his suffering and humility at the end strike a very different note. His physical power is gone, along with his sight, but he has grown in

Key quotation

Rochester of his marriage to Bertha: 'An agony of inward contempt masters me. I never loved, I never esteemed, I did not even know her.'
(p. 352)

Key quotation

'For the world's judgement – I wash my hands thereof. For man's opinion – I defy it.'
(p. 295)

Build critical skills

How does Charlotte Brontë's use of long words and abstract nouns in the passage below suggest to the reader that Rochester is uncomfortable with the course of action he has chosen?

'To attain this end, are you justified in overleaping an obstacle of custom – a mere conventional impediment which neither your conscience sanctifies nor your judgment approves?'
(p. 252)

moral stature – he admits to having been 'an irreligious dog' but has now experienced 'remorse, repentance, the wish for reconcilement to my Maker' (p. 514). Charlotte Brontë is signalling that he is now worthy of marrying Jane, and she herself acknowledges that 'he, in truth, loved me far too well and too tenderly to constitute himself my tyrant' (p. 507).

St John Rivers

St John Rivers, again presented through Jane's perceptions, goes in a different direction from Rochester, since he goes from kindness to coldness. His first action is to bring Jane in from the cold, but as readers we are increasingly aware that he is cold-hearted, calculating and committed above all to his own ambition. He says, but does not mean, 'I, for instance, am but dust and ashes' (p. 464).

St John, unlike Rochester, has a touch of a 'graceful Apollo' about him. He is 28–30 years old, with blue eyes and golden hair, 'tall, slender ... quite a straight classic nose; quite an Athenian mouth and chin' (p. 396). One of the book's themes, however, is that appearances are deceptive, and there is a gulf between his Christian commitment and his capacity for compassion. His actions, such as founding the new school in Morton, are correct and proper, but his feelings for his fellow human beings border on contempt. He even says, 'Know me to be what I am – a cold, hard man' (p. 432). He talks of missionary work as 'warfare' and Jane senses that he sees her only as a useful weapon in that war.

Build critical skills

How does Charlotte Brontë use this extract to suggest to the reader that St John does not have enough humanity to deserve Jane's love?

'I am simply, in my original state – stripped of that blood-bleached robe with which Christianity covers human deformity – a cold, hard, ambitious man.' (p. 432)

▲ St John Rivers and Jane (2011 film adaptation)

Key quotation

'...his face riveted the eye; it was like a Greek face, very pure in outline.'
(p. 396)

St John, although a missionary and therefore committed to helping others, despises people as 'feeble fellow worms' and has cold control over his emotions. The 'strictly restrained zeal' of his sermons comes across to Jane as increasingly chilling, while his self-control is both total and terrifying. He can captivate someone as shallow as Rosamond Oliver, but lacks the human warmth to appeal to Jane. He 'flushes' and 'kindles' at the sight of Rosamond Oliver, a 'perfect beauty' who clearly loves him, yet he will not allow himself to love someone who might not prove a good missionary. He puts ambition before emotion, and perceiving this enables Jane to reject him. St John's cold ferocity of purpose makes him almost inhuman ('no longer flesh, but marble') – he is 'as inexorable as death' about his 'missionary warfare'. Jane scorns the idea of love that St John Rivers offers because she has known the deeper love of Edward Rochester. After having Jane refuse to marry him, the author confirms her view of St John by having Jane ask her readers if they know the 'terror those cold people can put into the ice of their questions' (p. 475).

GRADE BOOSTER

When commenting on characters, the more detailed the analysis you provide that is relevant to the question asked, the more likely you are to meet the criteria for higher grades. It is better to say a lot about a little (i.e. one or two characters at specific moments) than a little about a lot (i.e. several characters across most of the novel), particularly for the higher grades.

Mr Brocklehurst

The way Charlotte Brontë introduces Mr Brocklehurst is a significant indication of the author's attitude: seen through Jane's childish eyes Mr Brocklehurst seemed 'a black pillar! ... straight, narrow, sable-clad shape standing erect on the rug; the grim face at the top was like a carved mask, placed above the shaft by way of capital' (p. 38). He is more a monster than a man of god. His interrogation of Jane focuses on the Bible and is used by the author to establish the distance between this alleged educator and the child he might be charged with educating – when Jane innocently and honestly comments that 'Psalms are not interesting', he claims, full of self-righteousness, that she has a 'wicked heart'.

Jane's fearful dislike is conveyed to us as readers and because Charlotte Brontë has 'tuned us in' so quickly to Mr Brocklehurst, we guess from his claim that 'Humility is a Christian grace' that he will soon be shown to be anything but humble. He is rapidly presented as a hypocrite of the worst sort, hiding his cruelty and avarice beneath a cloak of Christianity. When he talks of 'plain fare, simple attire' we can hear the author's message – he is just out to spend as little money as possible in keeping the Lowood girls alive.

Once she arrives at Lowood his sadistic treatment of Jane – putting her for hours on a 'pedestal of infamy' – means that readers can have no sympathy for him. Charlotte Brontë's true attitude to him is apparent when narrator Jane is made to say, 'Mr Brocklehurst again paused – perhaps overcome by his feelings' (p. 75). By this time the author has made sure that we appreciate the irony. His hypocrisy is reinforced by Charlotte Brontë through the inclusion of Mr Brocklehurst's spoilt daughters: while claiming of the Lowood girls that 'my mission is to

Build critical skills

How, through these words, does the author suggest that Mr Brocklehurst is a terrifying figure to a little girl?

'bending from the perpendicular, he installed his person in the arm-chair…' and 'What a face he had! … what a great nose! and what a mouth! and what large prominent teeth!' (p. 39)

mortify in these girls the lusts of the flesh' (p. 76), he indulges his daughters' every whim.

Mr Brocklehurst – the 'black marble clergyman' – looks fierce, abuses his authority and is Jane's feared and hated enemy. He is deservedly humiliated in the end when the deaths from typhoid draw public attention to the unhealthiness and inhumanity of Lowood, and is then 'aided in the discharge of his duties' by men of 'rather more enlarged and sympathising minds' (p. 99).

Helen Burns

Helen, like Charlotte's sister Maria, dies of tuberculosis while at school. The first time that Jane meets Helen, Charlotte Brontë signals to the reader that she will be short-lived. Jane hears Helen ('the sound of a cough behind me, made me turn my head') before she sees her. Helen befriends Jane and it is the support of Helen's smile that enables Jane to endure being shamed by having to stand on a stool for hours: narrator Jane says, 'What a smile! I remember it now … like a reflection from the aspect of an angel.' She adds that 'it lit up her marked lineaments, her thin face, her sunken gray eye' (p. 80), a description that suggests Helen's time on earth will not be long. Helen does not fear death – rather she sees it as 'an entrance to happiness – to glory', but knowledge that she is dying fills Jane with 'inexpressible sadness'.

Helen's response to Miss Scatcherd's unfair treatment is one of Christian humility: 'It is far better to endure patiently a smart which nobody feels but yourself, than to commit a hasty action whose evil consequences will extend to all connected with you' (p. 66). Helen tells Jane that: 'you are too impulsive, too vehement', but she is a true friend to younger Jane – 'Helen, at all times and under all circumstances, evinced for me a quiet and faithful friendship, which ill-humour never soured, nor irritation ever troubled' (p. 93). During the tea-and-cakes evening with Miss Temple, Jane is 'struck with wonder' at the breadth and depth of Helen's learning, which includes being able to read Latin.

Key quotation

Helen: 'Life appears to me too short to be spent in nursing animosity, or registering wrongs.' (p. 69)

Helen is shown to be exceptionally intelligent, consistently calm and a true Christian, full of forgiveness for others and illuminated from within by her belief. Jane is portrayed as a Christian but her belief is not like Helen's, whose focus is on God's love and the glory to come after this life. Charlotte Brontë makes the episode when Jane is with Helen on her deathbed poignant without being pathetic. Helen's faith is her inspiration and, characteristically, her last words are to ask if Jane is warm enough.

Key quotation

'I believe; I have faith; I am going to God.' (p. 97)

Despite being in the novel only briefly, Helen is an important character: she helps Jane towards spiritual maturity, she embodies Christianity in its best sense and she establishes religious attitudes as one of the major themes.

Miss Temple

Because Charlotte Brontë presents Miss Temple through Jane's youthful eyes, we feel about her as Jane does, that (as her name implies) she is worth worshipping: intelligent, cultured and kind, she exercised 'a controlling sense of awe' (p. 86). Miss Temple's characteristically thoughtful first words are: 'The child is very young to be sent alone.' When criticised by Mr Brocklehurst for issuing extra food, 'her brow settled gradually into petrified severity.'

Miss Temple is surprisingly sophisticated, given her role at Lowood, and 'had always something of serenity in her air, of state in her mien, of refined propriety in her language' (p. 86). The author makes sure that we do not miss how learned she is by having Jane marvel at her conversation with Helen.

She is courageous in tending the sick and sympathetic to her pupils, and she exonerates Jane from Mr Brocklehurst's charge of deceit. For Jane she comes to serve as mother, governess and companion.

Miss Temple marries a good man to live (it is implied) happily ever after. Virtue is rewarded and the author has given us evidence early in the novel that a woman does not have to be rich or noble to be worthy of admiration.

Key quotation

Jane acknowledges, 'to her instruction I owed the best part of my acquirements.'
(p. 100)

Build critical skills

'"The child is very young to be sent alone," said she, putting her candle down on the table. She considered me attentively for a minute or two, then further added –

"She had better be put to bed soon; she looks tired. Are you tired?" she asked, placing her hand on my shoulder.

"A little, ma'am."

"And hungry too, no doubt: let her have some supper before she goes to bed, Miss Miller. Is this the first time you have left your parents to come to school, my little girl?"

I explained to her that I had no parents.'
(p. 52)

How does Charlotte Brontë use dialogue here to reveal Miss Temple's character?

Blanche Ingram

Blanche is presented as Jane's opposite, with Rochester (as the Old Gypsy) as the judge of them both. Through the contrast between them the novel explores issues connected with attraction based on appearance

Key quotation

Blanche 'had a fine person, many brilliant attainments; but her mind was poor, her heart barren by nature.'
(p. 215)

and financial worth, or based on truer emotions reflecting inner worth. Blanche may be beautiful and well-bred but she is shallow, spiteful, vain, intellectually limited and has an undeserved sense of her own superiority. In Jane's (biased) view, Miss Ingram 'was a mark beneath jealousy'.

The moment that Charlotte Brontë's own view of Blanche is most obvious is when she nastily condemns governesses: 'half of them detestable and the rest ridiculous.' We do not need to know that Charlotte Brontë was a governess to know how the author expects readers to react to this – Blanche merits our contempt. Further evidence is that Blanche's interest in Rochester is for his position and property rather than his person. She deserves his acid comment that 'Her feelings are concentrated in one – pride; and that needs humbling' (p. 303).

The Reed family

Mrs Reed's character is suggested with her opening words: we suspect anyone who responds to a child's reasonable question with, 'there is something truly forbidding in a child taking up her elders in that manner' (p. 9). Charlotte Brontë uses Mrs Reed to establish an image of Jane's fierce independence by having her challenge Mrs Reed's conduct towards her – 'People think you are a good woman, but you are bad, hard-hearted. *You* are deceitful!' (p. 44). Her next appearance in the novel is on her deathbed. She is still rigid, unforgiving and unrepentant over Jane, although she admits that she was jealous of Mr Reed's affection for Jane and that she lied to John Eyre, telling him that Jane had died. Her death distresses no one, not even her daughters.

Build critical skills

In this extract, how does Charlotte Brontë convey the impression of Mrs Reed as a powerful but pitiless figure?

'...she was a woman of robust frame, square-shouldered and strong-limbed, not tall, and though stout, not obese; she had a somewhat large face, the under-jaw being much developed and very solid; her brow was low, her chin large and prominent ... under her light eyebrows glimmered an eye devoid of ruth.'
(p. 43)

John Reed is stupid, spoilt and a bully. His appearance matches his character and he is positively ugly: 'large and stout for his age with a dingy and unwholesome skin; thick lineaments in a spacious visage, heavy limbs and large extremities ... dim and bleared eye and flabby cheeks' (p. 12). Jane compares John Reed to tyrannical Roman emperors, and his path towards self-destruction starts early. He is kept away from school because of his 'delicate health' by a doting mother, who attributes his paleness to pining after home rather than to an excess of cakes and sweetmeats. Jane can escape into her imagination, but John has neither intelligence nor imagination. He is 'not quick either of vision or conception' and uses books as weapons, prizing their weight more than their words. He is vicious towards Jane, but cowardly, and before too long is dead from excessive indulgence. Not an important character, he is nevertheless Charlotte Brontë's early marker that there is not necessarily a link between social status and human worth.

When young, the two Reed sisters are comically different. Georgiana cares only about her looks, typically 'sat on a high stool, dressing her hair at the glass, and interweaving her curls with artificial flowers' (p. 36). Eliza, meanwhile, cares only about her lucre: she keeps chickens and sells the eggs – 'She had a turn for traffic, and a marked propensity for saving' (p. 36); 'Eliza would have sold the hair off her head if she could have made a handsome profit thereby' (p. 36). When older, they resent each other deeply. In Bessie's words, 'she and her sister lead a cat-and-dog life together; they are always quarrelling' (p. 108). Georgiana is buxom and brainless, Eliza skinny and self-absorbed. Georgiana has 'aspirations after dissipations to come' and cares what society thinks of her, while Eliza avoids society by seeking the consolation of solitariness in a convent. Having spent a month in their company, Jane reflects that, 'Eliza did not mortify me, nor Georgiana ruffle me.' Neither seems to mourn the loss of their brother or mother.

The Reed servants are minor characters. Abbot (we never know her first name) is unfeeling and unpleasant. Bessie Lee, however, is much more human: 'a slim young woman, with black hair, dark eyes, very nice features, and good, clear complexion; but she had a capricious and hasty temper' (p. 36). She reveals genuine care for Jane, especially on her last night at Gateshead Hall. Bessie features later in the novel when she seeks out Jane at Lowood and finds her 'quite a lady'. She updates Jane on the Reeds as well as commenting on her plain appearance. Jane tells us that 'Bessie Lee must, I think, have been a girl of good natural capacity, for she was smart in all she did, and had a remarkable knack of narrative' (p. 36).

GRADE BOOSTER

Most questions are not just about characters but are about how the author 'presents' characters. For example, the task might be to analyse how Charlotte Brontë presents a character in a particular extract and then in the novel as a whole. Because the task is focused on Charlotte Brontë's methods, not just on a character, you are expected to include analysis of language, structure, theme and chronological context. Examiners look for your personal interpretation of the characters and of their relationships with each other. For example, you might make the following comment: 'Charlotte Brontë has created contrasting pairs of characters, such as Rochester and St John Rivers, and the differences between them illuminate the nature of romantic love and clarify the choices facing Jane.' This shows that you have seen how characters relate to each other and provided a relevant and intelligent response to a character task, which reflects deeper understanding of ideas and of the novel as a whole.

Build critical skills

Charlotte Brontë created several of her characters as deliberate contrasts with each other: Rochester vs St John Rivers; Jane vs Blanche, Rosamond and Bertha; Mr Brocklehurst vs Miss Temple; and Georgiana vs Eliza Reed.

Find quotations by or about each pair of characters that signal that contrast.

GRADE FOCUS

Grade 5

To achieve a Grade 5, examiners expect you to focus on the question asked and to show clear understanding of how and why Charlotte Brontë uses language, form and structure to create characters, and when writing about how Charlotte Brontë presents and explores a character to make relevant points (e.g. 'Brontë demonstrates that Mr Brocklehurst is a religious hypocrite through . . .'). Remember that characters are the author's creations rather than real people, and include quotations from the text to prove your points.

Grade 8

To achieve a Grade 8, you need to demonstrate that you appreciate that characters are constructs, created and manipulated by Charlotte Brontë in order to have particular impact on her readers and to examine and evaluate the ways that she achieves this. You also need to point out how Brontë's characterisation helps to develop some of the main themes of the novel.

Your argument needs to be based on detailed textual evidence in the form of brief, well-integrated and well-chosen quotations.

REVIEW YOUR LEARNING

(Answers are given on p. 109.)

1. Who shows Jane at least a degree of kindness at Gateshead Hall?
2. Who befriends Jane at Lowood School?
3. What suggests most strongly that Mr Brocklehurst is a hypocrite?
4. How does the author suggest what Mr Rochester thinks of society and its conventions?
5. How does Charlotte Brontë show that Jane differs from Blanche Ingram?
6. What do you think of Mr Rochester's teasing of Jane before proposing to her?
7. Which two or three pairs of characters has Charlotte Brontë created as deliberate contrasts?
8. How does Charlotte Brontë show Jane's impression of St John Rivers changing over time?
9. How does Charlotte Brontë try to make it credible that Jane could still love blind and maimed Rochester?
10. Why do you think the final words of the novel are about St John Rivers?

Themes

Target your thinking

- What is a theme? (**AO1**, **AO3**)
- What are the main themes in *Jane Eyre*? (**AO1**, **AO3**)
- How are these themes presented and explored by Charlotte Brontë? (**AO2**)

A loose definition of a theme in fiction is that it is an idea that the author explores throughout the novel. Something that features only once or twice would not be sufficiently implanted in the mind of readers to be called a theme. There are several different ways of categorising the themes in *Jane Eyre*, and in any interpretation of literary themes there is bound to be some overlap, but the ideas below are returned to again and again:

- education
- religion
- romantic love
- the role of women

Although Charlotte Brontë was addressing the problems of a particular time and place, it can be argued that her themes have universality, which means that many of her concerns are still relevant to us today.

GRADE BOOSTER

Turn to the 'Top quotations' section, pp. 104-105, for short memorable quotations on the main themes. You will find it useful to have them at your fingertips in the examination.

Education

A theme that is introduced at the beginning of the novel, and returned to throughout, is education – how children are treated in families and schools by those with the responsibility for bringing them up. This was a real concern to Charlotte Brontë who suffered (as Jane does) in an awful residential school and who worked as a governess.

During her miserable time at Gateshead Hall, Jane endures 'a life of ceaseless reprimand' (p. 25) and unfair treatment. On the very first page we see Mrs Reed's unreasonable response to a reasonable question and learn that in her view education does not involve enquiry: 'Jane, I don't like cavillers or questioners ... until you can speak pleasantly, remain silent.' Jane's early education comes from books rather than from people; while hidden in the window seat her mind travels the world through her imagination with the help of *Bewick's Birds*, in which 'every picture told a story'. Significantly, it is a book that sparks her rebellion against John Reed's tyranny, since for him books are weapons rather than wonders.

Key quotation

Of Bewick's Birds: 'Each picture told a story; mysterious often to my undeveloped understanding and imperfect feelings, yet ever profoundly interesting.'
(p. 11)

Build critical skills

What does the passage below suggest to you about Mr Brocklehurst's idea of education?

'My second daughter, Augusta, went with her mama to visit the school, and on her return she exclaimed, "Oh, dear papa, how quiet and plain all the girls at Lowood look; with their hair combed behind their ears, and their long pinafores, and those little holland pockets outside their frocks,they are almost like poor people's children! and," said she, "they looked at my dress and mama's, as if they had never seen a silk gown before."'
(p. 41)

Key quotation

Mr Brocklehurst: 'you may indeed feed their vile bodies, but you little think how you starve their immortal souls!'
(p. 75)

Mr Brocklehurst's investigation of Jane's education is largely about the Bible, and the missing of meanings over how to avoid hell – 'I must keep in good health, and not die' (p. 39) is one of the rare moments of humour in the novel.

At Lowood, education is essentially about social control. Rather than celebrate individuality, the school routines and regulations seek to eliminate it: they were 'a congregation of girls of every age, from nine or ten to twenty ... uniformly dressed in brown stuff frocks of quaint fashion, and long holland pinafores' (p. 52). The compulsory hairstyle 'gave an air of oddity even to the prettiest'.

▲ Classroom scene from the 1944 film adaptation

Given that Lowood is based on the school that Charlotte herself attended, and where two of her sisters died, it is hardly surprising that readers are given an impression of harshness and hypocrisy. Mr Brocklehurst is responsible for both: he conceals the neglect of the girls under the cloak of Christian concern for their moral and spiritual welfare. His hypocrisy is highlighted not only by the contrast between his treatment of the girls and of his own spoilt daughters, but by the difference between his attitudes and those of Miss Temple. The browbeaten teachers reflect the atmosphere and attitudes, with Miss Scatcherd the most vindictive in her cruel treatment of Helen Burns. We look at the school through Jane's eyes and share her feelings, so the excruciating shame when she is stood on a stool for hours is burnt into a reader's mind as exemplifying all that is wrong with Lowood under Mr Brocklehurst.

Once Mr Brocklehurst is no longer in charge, the reformed Lowood becomes 'a truly useful and noble institution' and provides Jane with a good education. She in turn is a successful governess to Adèle (more effective than Charlotte Brontë was as a governess!) and a good teacher in Morton. She finds real satisfaction in her teaching there and admits that those who she initially undervalued as 'heavy-looking gaping rustics' prove to be sharp-witted, amiable and obliging, sometimes with 'natural politeness and innate self-respect'. The progress they make wins her admiration and she ends by liking and being liked by several of the girls. Fundamental to her success is that she actually cares for her charges: despite her patronising nineteenth-century comments (e.g. 'though it be but the regard of working people') and the speed with which she closes the school on inheriting a fortune, the Charlotte Brontë message on education is fairly clear – humanity and a capacity for empathy are essential to an effective teaching relationship.

Significantly, Charlotte Brontë has Jane ask near the end of the novel, 'You have not quite forgotten little Adèle, have you reader?' and when she discovers that Adèle is unhappy at her school she has her moved nearer to home and to a school that suits her. Education matters both to Charlotte Brontë and to her persona Jane.

Religion

Charlotte Brontë was a clergyman's daughter who was brought up by a fiercely religious aunt and eventually married a clergyman. Religion was inevitably much more a part of her life than it would necessarily be for a modern writer or reader, but she felt strongly that 'self-righteousness is not religion' and the novel paints a devastating picture of religious hypocrisy.

There are positive images of religion in the novel: for both Jane and Helen Burns religion is something private, personal and deeply felt. Helen Burns is portrayed as a genuinely religious figure. Her focus is on God's love and the glory to come after this life. Her eyes are inspired by a 'strange light' and her smile is 'angelic'. Her death is not portrayed as tragic since she is ready to die and says that she lives in calm, 'looking to the end', and that her belief 'makes eternity a rest – a mighty home, not a terror or an abyss' (p. 70). She says, 'by dying young I shall escape great sufferings.' She is calm and confident about going to heaven.

Jane herself often refers to God, but Charlotte Brontë hints that Jane is being idolatrous in worshipping Rochester so much: she has Jane say, 'I could not, in those days, see God for His creature: of whom I had made an idol' (p. 316).

When wandering in the wilderness of the countryside she is shunned by human society yet feels that, 'Nature seemed to me benign and good ...

Build critical skills

The words in the passage below are those of the character Jane, rather than of her creator, but terms like 'torpid' and 'hopelessly dull' jar our modern ears. Jane admits that she was wrong, so how might Charlotte Brontë have expected her readers to react?

'Some time elapsed before, with all my efforts, I could comprehend my scholars and their nature. Wholly untaught, with faculties quite torpid, they seemed to me hopelessly dull; and, at first sight, all dull alike: but I soon found I was mistaken. There was a difference amongst them as amongst the educated.'
(p. 422)

Key quotation

Helen: 'I believe; I have faith: I am going to God.'
(p. 97)

We know that God is everywhere; but certainly we feel his presence most when His works are on the grandest scale spread before us, and it is in the unclouded night-sky where His worlds wheel their silent course that we read clearest His infinitude, His omnipotence, His omnipresence' (p. 373).

Key quotation

'I will keep the law given by God; sanctioned by man.'
(p. 365)

She seeks to act as God would wish, especially when Rochester asks her to go away with him, but not as his wife: she tells herself that 'Laws and principles are not for times when there is no temptation: they are for such moments as this when body and soul rise in mutiny against their rigour' (p. 365). Even Rochester, formerly 'an irreligious dog', finally begins to 'experience remorse, repentance, the wish for reconcilement to my Maker' (p. 514).

The representatives of organised religion, however, do not come out well. So much so that one contemporary reviewer condemned the novel as 'an anti-Christian tract'. Mr Brocklehurst is depicted as a Christian hypocrite of the first order, mouthing pieties to maximise his own profits. Even saintly Helen Burns damns him with the faintest of praise – 'He is a clergyman, and is said to do a great deal of good.' His hypocrisy is never more apparent than when criticising Miss Temple for taking pity on the hungry girls at Lowood: 'Oh Madam, when you put bread and cheese, instead of burnt porridge, into these children's mouths, you may indeed feed their vile bodies, but you little think how you starve their immortal souls!' (p. 75). As readers we feel that justice has been done when he is replaced as Principal of Lowood by men 'who knew how to combine reason with strictness, comfort with economy, compassion with uprightness' (p. 100).

Eliza Reed's decision to enter a convent is portrayed as a selfish avoidance of life, rather than something admirable. Jane's reaction to hearing that Eliza is likely to enter a nunnery and 'embrace the tenets of Rome' is to think, 'The vocation will fit you to a hair ... much good may it do you!' (p. 279).

Key quotation

St John Rivers: 'It is the cause of God I advocate: it is under His standard I enlist you.'
(p. 468)

St John is presented as a subtler example of a Christian hypocrite. He wears the mask of a principled Evangelical Christian, but his icy dedication is to his own ambition, not to his flock. His reserved, brooding nature means that he feels neither comfort nor calm despite his zealous Christianity. St John's attitude to Christianity shows in his sermons, which despite their power have a bitterness and hardness beneath their 'strictly restrained zeal'. He feels that 'his heart is laid upon a sacred altar' and in his 'Christian stoicism' will not let himself love beautiful, doting Rosamond Oliver. Charlotte Brontë does not invite her readers to admire his self-denial or the missionary commitment, which is 'My foundation laid on earth for a mansion in heaven' (p. 431). Like Jane, we initially feel impressed by his hospitality, his appearance ('his face riveted the eye') and his calm thoughtfulness, but eventually come to see him as cold-hearted and calculating.

Romantic love

Jane Eyre is a love story, but is not just a love story: it presents personal love and passion, but does so in the context of the major ideas of the time, such as religion, education, the structure of society and the freedom of the individual.

At the heart of the novel is the story of the love between the poor, plain, orphaned Jane and the aristocratic but deeply damaged Rochester. Their first meeting is constructed by the author to be anything but love at first sight: it is only because Rochester does *not* seem too handsome or heroic that Jane is calm enough to offer him help. Nevertheless, there is a tangible sense of the impact that this man 'of middle height and considerable breadth of chest' has on her. He has 'a dark face, with stern features and a heavy brow; his eyes and gathered eyebrows looked ireful and thwarted' (p. 134), and Jane later says, 'your sternness has a power beyond beauty' (p. 283).

In the early nineteenth century it was often assumed (usually by men!) that women did not have deep intellects and could not cope with powerful emotions. Hence the outcry in some quarters when *Jane Eyre*, with its intelligent, passionate heroine, was published. Respectable women were not supposed to experience feelings of sexual desire, but part of Jane's development is the growth of her undeniably sexual feelings for Mr Rochester. She is very aware of his power and masculinity and at times the intensity of her emotion is powerfully conveyed: 'a hand of fiery iron grasped my vitals. Terrible moment: full of struggle, blackness, burning' (p. 363). Sexual feelings are not made explicit, but they are there in the imagery of burning fires of passion and in the figure of Bertha.

▲ Jane and Rochester in the 2011 film adaptation

Key quotation

Jane: 'Not a human being that ever lived could wish to be loved better than I was loved.'
(p. 363)

Before long Jane acknowledges to the reader that she has 'learnt to love Mr Rochester: I could not unlove him now, merely because I found that he had ceased to notice me' (p. 215). We are invited to share Jane's perspectives, and when she thinks that Mr Rochester is going to marry Blanche Ingram – 'because her rank and connexions suited him' – she does not condemn him, but she does affirm that she would marry only for love. Despite his flirting with Blanche, Rochester is impatient with superficiality in appearance or behaviour. He is 'the very devil' to women who 'please me only by their faces' and overall his perceptiveness about people is a good match with Jane's. He has no time for social pretensions or hypocrisy. He loves Jane for herself, regardless of her station in society. The fact that she is a governess and therefore his servant does not influence his perception of her or his love for her. If anything, the fact that she is so unused to society adds to her appeal for him: 'Station! station! – your station is in my heart, and on the necks of those who would insult you, now or hereafter' (p. 304).

Build critical skills

How does Charlotte Brontë's use of dialogue increase the intensity of emotion in this passage?

'"Jane, do you mean to go one way in the world, and to let me go another?"

"I do."

"Jane" (bending towards and embracing me), "do you mean it now?"

"I do."

"And now?" softly kissing my forehead and cheek.

"I do," extricating myself from restraint rapidly and completely.

"Oh, Jane, this is bitter! This – this is wicked. It would not be wicked to love me."

"It would to obey you."'

(p. 364)

Charlotte Brontë uses Jane as her mouthpiece (persona) to suggest that a love that is not passionate, such as that of St John Rivers, is not love at all. By contrast, her passion for Rochester seems all-consuming: she says, 'My future husband was becoming to me my whole world' and he temporarily replaces God – 'I could not, in those days, see God for His creature: of whom I had made an idol' (p. 316). Nevertheless, she retains a sense of morality that means she is determined to 'keep the law given by God' regarding the sanctity of marriage. Rochester, given his contempt for convention – 'unheard-of combinations of circumstances demand unheard-of rules' – has no such reservations and wants Jane to flee with him to the south of France. His passion is so selfish and all-consuming that he is ready to put the reputation and well-being of his beloved Jane at risk in order to be with her. There is almost a suggestion that uncontrolled sexuality, evident in his first marriage as well as in his desire for Jane, results in madness and destruction, and that Rochester's immoral passion has to be tamed before marriage with the heroine is possible. His maiming in the Thornfield fire could be seen as the symbolic punishment the author metes out for his fierily passionate feelings.

Rochester first admits his love for Jane only after Charlotte Brontë has established their matching equality of spirit (as opposed to social standing) in the mind of the reader. Jane at her most passionate, having misunderstood Rochester's intentions, declares, 'it is my spirit that addresses your spirit; just as if both had passed through the grave, and we stood at God's feet, equal – as we are!' (p. 292).

Eventually we see again that theirs is indeed a marriage of 'true minds' – of people who are independent in spirit. It is because of their respect for each other that they can be truly happy together when their physical situations are so different.

Key quotation

Jane to Rochester: 'your sternness has a power beyond beauty'
(p. 283)

Key quotation

Rochester: 'My bride is here … because my equal is here, and my likeness. Jane, will you marry me?'
(p. 294)

The role of women

In her Preface to the second edition of *Jane Eyre*, Charlotte Brontë writes of 'the warped system of things.' One aspect of that warped system about which she felt very strongly was the role and treatment of women. Women's lives were largely determined by men, whether fathers, husbands or legislators. No wonder Charlotte (thinly disguised as Jane) wrote of women that, 'It is thoughtless to condemn them, or laugh at them, if they seek to do more or learn more than custom has pronounced necessary for their sex' (p. 130). For many 'genteel' women, unless they had the education to become governesses, marriage was the only way to escape the family home, and this depended on parental consent as Charlotte found to her cost a few years after she wrote *Jane Eyre*.

Charlotte Brontë saw herself as making the case for change on behalf of millions of women who were 'in silent revolt against their lot'. Plain Jane's journey from despised dependent relative to lady of independent mind and means showed that a heroine need not be pretty to make progress. It also challenged Victorian assumptions about the place of women in a society in which women were very much second-class citizens who did not have the vote, were virtually their husband's property and had hardly any career opportunities. Even Blanche Ingram, despite her social position and her beauty, has no choice but to put herself up for sale in the marriage market, available to anyone rich enough to pay a suitable price.

Build critical skills

It is significant that Charlotte Brontë did not write, 'Reader, he married me.' Instead it is, 'Reader, I married him.' How does the order of words and the use of pronouns suggest that the power here lies with the woman?

In the novel Charlotte Brontë has created Jane as a female figure who challenges the conventions that kept women subservient: she rebels against bullying; she earns her own living; she refuses to become Rochester's mistress although she loves him deeply; she refuses to marry St John and defies convention by marrying a blind cripple. Above all, she maintains her independence of mind and action. When a desperate Rochester asks, 'Who in the world cares for you?', she responds indomitably, '*I* care for myself. The more solitary, the more friendless, the more unsustained I am, the more I will respect myself' (p. 365). That was almost revolutionary by Victorian standards.

There are other admirable women in the novel, notably Miss Temple, but by contrast there is also Bertha, a woman beyond Rochester's control. In her there is an image of a woman of sexualised savagery, whose power is dangerous indeed. The implication may be that if women can control their emotions (as Jane does) then everything is possible, but if they lose control then that way madness lies.

The most powerful statement of the novelist's views on women (given by her mouthpiece/persona, Jane) comes in Chapter 12:

> 'Women are supposed to be very calm generally: but women feel just as men feel; they need exercise for their faculties, and a field for their efforts as much as their brothers do; they suffer from too rigid a restraint, too absolute a stagnation, precisely as men would suffer; and it is narrow-minded in their more privileged fellow-creatures to say that they ought to confine themselves to making puddings and knitting stockings, to playing on the piano and embroidering bags. It is thoughtless to condemn them, or laugh at them, if they seek to do more or learn more than custom has pronounced necessary for their sex.'
>
> (pp. 129–130)

Not many men thought that way in the 1840s, so it was not surprising that before long the writer of the novel was revealed to be a woman.

GRADE BOOSTER

Examination questions may ask you to consider how Charlotte Brontë uses a particular character to present a theme. For example, how does Charlotte Brontë present the theme of education through Mr Brocklehurst and Miss Temple? Learn to think of characters in this way.

GRADE FOCUS

Grade 5

To achieve Grade 5, students will reveal a clear understanding of the key themes of the novel and of how Charlotte Brontë uses language, form and structure to explore them, supported by appropriate references to the text.

Grade 8

To achieve Grade 8, students will be able to examine and evaluate the key themes of the novel, analysing the ways that Charlotte Brontë uses language, form and structure to explore them. Comments will be supported by carefully chosen and well-integrated references to the text.

REVIEW YOUR LEARNING

(Answers are given on p. 109.)

1. What is a theme?
2. What are the main themes of *Jane Eyre*?
3. How is the theme of education introduced?
4. Which situations contribute to the theme of education?
5. How is the theme of religion introduced?
6. Which characters contribute to the theme of religion?
7. Which images are associated with the theme of love?
8. How does Jane demonstrate her independence?
9. How does Charlotte Brontë portray the upper classes?
10. What methods does Charlotte Brontë use to convey her thoughts about the place of women in society?

Language, style and analysis

Target your thinking

- Which literary traditions influenced Charlotte Brontë? (**AO2**)
- Why does Charlotte Brontë use a narrator to tell the story? (**AO2**)
- What are some of Charlotte Brontë's typical language techniques? (**AO2**)

GRADE BOOSTER

Remember: it is not enough simply to identify the methods used by a writer; you must explore the effects on the reader of the use of these features.

When analysing language and style, the Assessment Objective with which we are most concerned is AO2, which refers to the writer's methods and is usually signalled in an exam question by the word 'how'. It is about the ways in which writers inform and influence the reader's understanding of plot, character and themes.

Examiners report that AO2 is often the Assessment Objective handled least well by students in the examination. For example, candidates who fail to address AO2 effectively often write about the characters in a novel as if they were real people involved in real events, rather than analysing them as 'constructs' or creations of the writer. To succeed with AO2, you must deal effectively with the writer's use of language, form and structure. Turn to page 34 for analysis of the structure of *Jane Eyre*.

Form

The form of a novel refers to the choice that the writer makes in terms of how she tells the story, in other words the viewpoint. When *Jane Eyre: An Autobiography* was published in 1847, it was claiming to be the autobiography of a woman called Jane Eyre, edited by a man named Currer Bell. In fact it was a work of fiction written wholly by Charlotte Brontë, but it does draw on aspects of her own life and character. It has elements from other types of writing as well as autobiography. Those types include romance, mystery, Gothic horror and the coming-of-age novel (or *Bildungsroman*), which tracks the emotional and spiritual development of a young person.

Autobiographical elements

When Charlotte Brontë wrote her novel, her readers would have known about pseudo-autobiographies. One of the most famous was Jonathan Swift's *Gulliver's Travels*, which is mentioned in the novel. *Gulliver's Travels* is a work of total invention involving travel to strange places such as Lilliput (where the people are tiny) and Brobdingnag (where the people are giants), but is supposedly the true accounts of a traveller called Lemuel Gulliver.

Using the form of an autobiography, and therefore writing in the first person, has great advantages for a writer: it means that she can control what the first-time reader sees, because we look through Jane's eyes and share her thoughts and feelings. We are, like Jane, increasingly curious about the strange sounds and happenings at Thornfield Hall. We may be convinced that there is some 'mystery', but we are as puzzled as Jane. When she guesses (wrongly, but reasonably) that Grace Poole is the likely culprit for starting the first fire, we share her bewilderment when Grace Poole acts as if nothing had happened – 'so much was I occupied in puzzling my brains over the enigmatical character of Grace Poole' (p. 181).

Had Charlotte Brontë chosen to tell the story without a first-person narrator, the narrative would have had far less immediacy. Even at a mundane moment we as readers are there with Jane: 'I was now in the schoolroom; Adèle was drawing; I bent over her and directed her pencil. She looked up with a sort of start' (p. 182). When emotions are involved, the sense of a shared experience is even greater: we are not just there with Jane, we are inside her head – 'Every good, true, vigorous feeling I have gathers impulsively round him. I know I must conceal my sentiments: must smother hope; I must remember that he cannot care much for me' (p. 204).

At times this personal voice sounds very much like the author speaking from experience: after her mother's death Charlotte Brontë was sent to a residential school for the daughters of the clergy, where two of her sisters died of consumption. It is not naïve little Jane's voice saying of Lowood, 'Semi-starvation and neglected colds had predisposed most of the pupils to receive infection: forty-five out of the eighty girls lay ill at one time' (p. 91) – this is Charlotte Brontë herself, using the persona (i.e. mouthpiece) of an older Jane Eyre to convey her remembered resentment.

Narrative voice

One result of Charlotte Brontë's choice of an autobiographical form is that the novel becomes a continuing conversation between the reader and the voice of the storyteller, usually that of Jane as an older woman. At a series of significant points, particularly towards the end of the novel, that conversation becomes a direct address to the reader, as in the examples below:

> 'A new chapter in a novel is something like a new scene in a play; and when I draw up the curtain this time, reader, you must fancy you see a room in the George Inn at Millcote.'
>
> (p. 111)

Build critical skills

What effect on you as a reader does the use of the first person have in the passage below? The passage comes after St John Rivers reveals to Jane that she is a relative and an heiress.

'I walked fast through the room: I stopped, half suffocated with the thoughts that rose faster than I could receive, comprehend, settle them: – thoughts of what might, could, would, and should be, and that ere long. I looked at the blank wall: it seemed a sky thick with ascending stars – every one lit me to a purpose or delight. Those who had saved my life, whom, till this hour, I had loved barrenly, I could now benefit. They were under a yoke – I could free them: they were scattered – I could reunite them: the independence, the affluence which was mine, might be theirs too.'

(p. 445)

> 'It is a fine thing, reader, to be lifted in a moment from indigence to wealth – a very fine thing; but not a matter one can comprehend, or consequently enjoy, all at once.'
>
> (p. 441)

> About blinded Rochester: 'And reader, do you think I feared him in his blind ferocity? – if you do, you little know me.'
>
> (p. 498)

And most famously,

> 'Reader, I married him.'
>
> (p. 517)

Build critical skills

What effect on you as a reader does the use of a child-like narrator have in the passage below? Jane has been found reading behind the curtain and commanded to come out by John Reed.

'I came out immediately, for I trembled at the idea of being dragged forth…' (p. 12)

Charlotte Brontë ensures that readers will identify with Jane in two ways: by making her the narrator through whose eyes we see people and events, and by giving her characteristics that readers find engaging. Some of her traits emerge early on during her childhood: she is strong-willed, has a fierce sense of justice, an independent spirit and a capacity for passion. By the time she marries Mr Rochester, still only a young woman, we know that she is intelligent, courageous, creative, loyal and loving. Surprisingly for such a modestly conventional character, she successfully challenges a range of social conventions and is eminently worthy of the conventional ending in which she lives happily ever after.

Having Jane as her persona (i.e. the imagined figure behind which she conceals herself) enables Charlotte Brontë to concentrate on key episodes in Jane's development and to summarise or ignore less important periods. For example, at Lowood, after the death of Helen Burns, Jane tells the reader that, 'I now pass a space of eight years almost in silence' (p. 99).

Charlotte Brontë uses the voice of Jane Eyre as the narrator. At times that voice is of an older woman recounting her childhood, as in 'child as I was.' At other times, however, it is as if we are looking through the eyes of a child: 'I mounted into the window-seat: gathering up my feet, I sat cross-legged, like a Turk' (p. 10). The comparison with a Turk (an exotic, romantic figure in a child's imagination) is perhaps not one that would be made by an older woman.

Gothic fiction or **Gothic horror**: a genre (type) of literature that features elements such as mystery, blood, atmospheric buildings, sensational events and passionate feelings. It was popularised by the English author Horace Walpole, with his 1764 novel (which Charlotte Brontë would have read), *The Castle of Otranto: A Gothic Story*.

Gothic elements

A vein of the supernatural runs through the novel: for example, Rochester frequently refers to Jane as being 'fairy-like' or, on one occasion, 'She comes from the other world – from the abode of people who are dead' (p. 282). The supernatural elements add to the **Gothic** feel of the story. They make the love between Rochester and Jane seem special, almost magical, and like something beyond ordinary life. While she is at Moor House, Jane uncannily senses Rochester's despairing cry from many miles away. At times, Charlotte Brontë creates a deliberately mysterious and macabre atmosphere, especially around Bertha's madness – 'Here then was I in the third story, fastened into one of its mystic cells; night around me; a pale and bloody spectacle under my eyes and hands; a murderess hardly separated from me by a single door…' (p. 242). The author uses recurrent images of darkness, often lit by flickering flames, and this culminates in the fire that destroys Thornfield and leaves Rochester maimed and blinded. Monster-like, he asks, 'Am I hideous, Jane?', but the monstrousness of the situation has been calmed and this is a monster whom she has learned to love.

▲ Scene from the 1970 TV film adaptation, with Bertha in the foreground

Build critical skills

What features of Gothic writing do you note in the passage below? What effect do they have on a reader?

'What crime was this, that lived incarnate in this sequestered mansion, and could neither be expelled nor subdued by the owner? – what mystery, that broke out, now in fire and now in blood, at the deadest hours of night? What creature was it, that, masked in an ordinary woman's face and shape, uttered the voice, now of a mocking demon, and anon of a carrion-seeking bird of prey?'
(p. 243)

Romantic love

Jane Eyre is notable for the intensity, and sometimes the simplicity, of its language about passionate emotions: at one point a desperate Jane says, 'I am not talking to you now through the medium of custom, conventionalities, nor even of mortal flesh; – it is my spirit that addresses your spirit; just as if both had passed through the grave, and we stood at God's feet, equal – as we are!' (p. 292). In a calmer moment she thinks aloud, powerfully but simply: 'I turned my lips to the hand that lay on my shoulder. I loved him very much – more than I could trust myself to say – more than words had power to express' (p. 304). (See 'Themes', p. 53, for more on romantic love.)

Key quotation

'a hand of fiery iron grasped my vitals. Terrible moment: full of struggle, blackness, burning!'
(p. 363)

Language features

Sentence structure

Although some of the sentence structures in *Jane Eyre* may seem complicated to a modern reader, the text was typical of its time. When she wants to move the story on, Charlotte Brontë writes quite simply, but many of the sentences are long because Charlotte Brontë wants to weave a web of connected ideas for readers instead of presenting separate ideas in short statements.

The extract below is from Rochester's words near the end of the novel:

> 'Who can tell what a dark, dreary, hopeless life I have dragged on for months past? Doing nothing, expecting nothing; merging night in day; feeling but the sensation of cold when I let the fire go out, of hunger when I forgot to eat: and then a ceaseless sorrow, and, at times, a very delirium of desire to hold my Jane again.'
>
> (p. 504)

Build critical skills

What effect does the wording of Rochester's proposal have on the reader?

'You – you strange, you almost unearthly thing! – I love you as my own flesh. You – poor and obscure, and small and plain as you are – I entreat to accept me as a husband.'
(p. 294)

The first sentence is a question and the author uses alliteration with repetition of 'd' at the start of 'dark, dreary' and 'dragging' to convey what a drawn-out, depressing time Rochester has spent. The second sentence, in which Rochester answers his own question, is 46 words long, but its length has a function: it enables Charlotte Brontë to plant a sequence of ideas in the reader's mind almost simultaneously. Rochester was experiencing all these feelings at once, and the nearest the author can get to helping readers share that experience is to include them all in the same sentence so that they are all in our minds, before the full stop allows us to pause for thought.

Often, as in the passage below, the movement of a sentence tracks the movements of Jane's actions and thoughts. You do not need to use elaborate technical terms to explain exactly which parts of speech or linguistic features are used – what matters is that you show you have noted and responded to the way words are used and the impact that this has on readers.

> '... I used to rush into strange dreams at night: dreams many-coloured, agitated, full of the ideal, the stirring, the stormy—dreams where, amidst unusual scenes, charged with adventure, with agitating risk and romantic chance, I still again and again met Mr. Rochester, always at some exciting crisis; and then the sense of being in his arms, hearing his voice, meeting his eye, touching his hand and cheek, loving him, being loved by him—the hope of passing a lifetime at his side, would be renewed, with all its first force and fire. Then I awoke.'
>
> (p. 423)

Look at the way words are used in the first sentence (which in total is 143 words long!), and at the contrast with the three-word sentence that follows. The first sentence recreates Jane's many-coloured dream for the reader: a dream full of ideas (nouns) like 'adventure', 'risk', 'chance', but nouns made more powerful by the accompanying adjectives: 'agitating risk', 'romantic chance'. Once Mr Rochester appears, it is the verbs that take over – 'being in his arms, hearing his voice, meeting his eye, touching his hand and cheek, loving him, being loved by him...' The dreams culminate in the alliterative excitement of 'first force and fire' but then the reader is, like Jane, jolted awake with 'Then I awoke' – an extraordinary contrast in terms of **syntax**.

Syntax: grammar; sentence construction.

Tense

Most of the novel is written using the past tense, but occasionally, during times of heightened emotion, the present tense is used to take out the distancing of time and to make events and feelings more immediate. An example is when Jane returns from Gateshead Hall to Thornfield: 'I see the narrow stile with stone steps; and I see – Mr Rochester sitting there, a book and a pencil in his hand; he is writing... Well, he is not a ghost; yet every nerve I have is unstrung' (p. 281).

Dialogue

Much of what happens in the novel is conveyed through dialogue. The author presents the words as if they are being spoken, rather than describing what was said. Charlotte Brontë is writing as an older Jane Eyre, and she could have opted for a (boring) style of *He said... She said...* for every conversation. She chose not to do that. Instead, she presents the dialogue in a way that enables us to 'listen in' to what is being said as if we were there too.

Build critical skills

What effect does Charlotte Brontë's use of sentence structure in the passage below have on readers? Jane is terrified, shut in the red room at night.

'My heart beat thick, my head grew hot; a sound filled my ears, which I deemed the rushing of wings: something seemed near me; I was oppressed, suffocated: endurance broke down ... I rushed to the door and shook the lock in desperate effort.'
(p. 21)

Build critical skills

The passage below is John Reed speaking to Jane. What effect on you as a reader does the use of dialogue have here?

'"What were you doing behind the curtain?" he asked.

"I was reading."

"Show the book."'

(p. 13)

'"You, Jane, I must have you for my own – entirely my own. Will you be mine? Say yes, quickly."

"Mr Rochester, let me look at your face: turn to the moonlight."

"Why?"

"Because I want to read your countenance – turn!"

"There! You will find it scarcely more legible than a crumpled, scratched page. Read on: only make haste, for I suffer."'

(p. 294)

Dialogue is also a way to increase the realism of a conversation by including local dialect. The most obvious example is Hannah at Moor House who, having said, 'You munnut think too hardly of me', acknowledges that Jane is 'a raight down dacent little crater' (p. 393).

Symbolism

Symbolism: when a word, image or character carries a wider meaning as well as its literal meaning.

The most obvious **symbol** in the novel is the great horse-chestnut tree in the Thornfield orchard. It symbolises the love between Jane and Rochester: when it writhes and groans in the roaring wind, we anticipate trouble ahead for the lovers. When it is struck by lightning and split in half, the message is unmistakable, and the link is made explicit by maimed Rochester.

Names

Names matter in the novel.

- None matters more than (plain) Jane **Eyre**. Charlotte Brontë knew of a local Yorkshire family called Eyre, whose house had contained a madwoman. The name also has the sound of 'air' and 'heir', both resonant when Jane is often referred to as a 'fairy' and indeed is the heir to her Uncle John's fortune.
- Miss **Temple** is an example of a character whose name reflects her qualities: she is worshipped by Jane, and with good reason.
- Helen **Burns** dies of a fever (consumption), but also burns with desire to go to heaven.
- The **Reed** family is swayed by every fashionable wind that blows.
- **St John Rivers** has a name, that of St John the Apostle, that signals he is a disciple, but he is carried on the current of his own ambition.
- The name **Rochester** (less obviously) has overtones of a fortress, but the names Rochester creates to tease Jane are the nearest thing to humour that he manages – Mrs Dionysius **O'Gall** of **Bitternutt Lodge**.
- **Blanche**, ironically, is not pale at all, except for her clothes.
- **Lowood**, as the name suggests, is unhealthily low-lying.
- **Thornfield Hall** has dangerously thorny thickets of emotion.

People

Charlotte Brontë often uses physical description to suggest character. For example, John Reed's physical unpleasantness reflects his unpleasant character – he is 'large and stout for his age, with a dingy and unwholesome skin' (p. 12). A contrasting use of the technique is Miss Temple: 'Let the reader add, to complete the picture, refined features; a complexion if pale, clear; and a stately air and carriage, and he will have, at least as clearly as words can give it, a correct idea of the exterior of Miss Temple' (p. 57).

Jane has been given the skill of her creator in summing up characters concisely. Blanche Ingram is 'showy, but she was not genuine', while Jane describes and dismisses the Lowood teachers thus: 'none of whom precisely pleased me; for the stout one was a little coarse, the dark one not a little fierce, the foreigner harsh and grotesque, and Miss Miller, poor thing! looked purple, weather-beaten and over-worked' (p. 56).

Build critical skills

How does Charlotte Brontë create a negative image of Eliza Reed in the mind of the reader?

'Two young ladies appeared before me; one very tall, almost as tall as Miss Ingram—very thin too, with a sallow face and severe mien. There was something ascetic in her look, which was augmented by the extreme plainness of a straight-skirted, black stuff dress, a starched linen collar, hair combed away from the temples, and the nun-like ornament of a string of ebony beads and a crucifix. This I felt sure was Eliza, though I could trace little resemblance to her former self in that elongated and colourless visage.'

(p. 263)

There are other characters, however, whose inner state is not matched by their outward appearance. The most obvious examples are Rochester and St John Rivers: the former's forbidding appearance belies his inner sensitivity, while the latter, despite looking like a Greek god with blue eyes and fair hair, has a heart of ice.

Places

Charlotte Brontë gives each place a distinct character, with emotional overtones. Often the weather links with the situation and emotion in what is known as **pathetic fallacy**.

Pathetic fallacy: when the weather or nature is used to reflect someone's feelings or mood.

- The novel's opening paragraphs convey a sense of the writer's feelings of rejection and sadness in an unfeeling world. The chill wind and penetrating rain match the emotional coldness of Gateshead Hall.

Build critical skills

What impression does this description of Ferndean create in the mind of the reader?

'The manor-house of Ferndean was a building of considerable antiquity, moderate size, and no architectural pretensions, deep buried in a wood.' (p. 496)

- On Jane's entry into Lowood, 'Rain, wind and darkness filled the air; nevertheless, I dimly discerned a wall before me and a door open in it' (p. 51).
- At Thornfield, 'candle-light gleamed from one curtained bow-window; all the rest were dark' but, within, 'a cosy and agreeable picture presented itself to my view' (p. 113).
- At Moor House: 'The light was yet there, shining dim but constant through the rain' (p. 380).

Imagery

Authors use imagery to create mental pictures for their readers. Charlotte Brontë makes Jane an imaginative, passionate and emotional character and uses imagery to convey her feelings. For example, after being assaulted by the 'tyrant' John Reed and shut in the red room, she recalls, 'my blood was still warm; the mood of the revolted slave was still bracing me with its bitter vigour' (p. 18). The images of tyranny and slavery link Jane's unjust sufferings with the woes of the world.

At Gateshead Hall Jane's actual world offers her no comfort or joy, but books like *Bewick's Birds* provide images that are beyond her daily world: 'Each picture told a story, mysterious often to my undeveloped understanding and imperfect feelings, yet ever profoundly interesting' (p. 11). These images of other worlds are 'Like all the half-comprehended notions that float dim through children's brains, but strangely impressive.' Those images will recur in her paintings later in the novel, and in her dreams. Dreams are not images in themselves, but Jane's dreams are full of images (often of children or the sea) that relate to her state of mind.

Build critical skills

How does Charlotte Brontë use this account of a dream to suggest Jane's state of mind?

'During all my first sleep, I was following the windings of an unknown road; total obscurity environed me; rain pelted me; I was burdened with the charge of a little child: a very small creature, too young and feeble to walk, and which shivered in my cold arms, and wailed piteously in my ear. I thought, sir, that you were on the road a long way before me; and I strained every nerve to overtake you, and made effort on effort to utter your name and entreat you to stop – but my movements were fettered, and my voice still died away inarticulate; while you, I felt, withdrew farther and farther every moment.' (p. 324)

Key images in *Jane Eyre* are fire and darkness, which often occur together. The fire is both actual (Bertha twice sets fire to Thornfield) and metaphorical – the fire of passionate sexuality between Jane and

Rochester, which contrasts with the iciness of St John Rivers. When Jane realises that she must leave Rochester, 'a hand of fiery iron grasped my vitals. Terrible moment: full of struggle, blackness, burning!' (p. 363). This sounds like the fires of hell, and Charlotte Brontë could be suggesting that, in accordance with the morality of England at the time, such burning passion amounted to a sin that deserved punishment.

Similes and metaphors

When writing about an extract from the novel, either the one on the exam paper or a quotation that you remember, it is useful to look out for examples of **similes** and **metaphors**, and to discuss their impact on readers. Both similes and metaphors create mental images for readers. In the quotation in the previous paragraph, did you notice the power of the metaphor, with pain compared to a fiery hand? Look at the passage in the 'Build critical skills' box on this page, where Charlotte Brontë uses similes rather than metaphors.

Simile: a comparison using the words 'as' or 'like'.

Metaphor: a comparison that doesn't use 'like' or 'as', but instead says something is something else.

Build critical skills

What do the similes in this passage about his time in the West Indies suggest about Rochester's state of mind?

'The air was like sulphur-steams – I could find no refreshment anywhere. Mosquitoes came buzzing in and hummed sullenly round the room; the sea, which I could hear from thence, rumbled dull like an earthquake – black clouds were casting up over it; the moon was setting in the waves, broad and red, like a hot cannon-ball – she threw her last bloody glance over a world quivering with the ferment of tempest. I was physically influenced by the atmosphere and scene.'

(p. 354)

GRADE FOCUS

Grade 5

To achieve a Grade 5, students will show a clear appreciation of the methods Charlotte Brontë uses to create effects for the reader, supported by appropriate references to the text.

Grade 8

To achieve a Grade 8, students will explore and analyse the methods that Charlotte Brontë uses to create effects for the reader, supported by carefully chosen and well-integrated references to the text.

REVIEW YOUR LEARNING

(Answers are given on pp. 109–110.)

1 What type of book was *Jane Eyre* described as when it was first published?
2 What are the advantages of first-person narration?
3 How does Charlotte Brontë use the appearance of John Reed to suggest his character?
4 Where does Charlotte Brontë use weather (pathetic fallacy) to indicate mood?
5 What do names like Reed, Burns and Temple suggest about these characters?
6 How does Charlotte Brontë use fire as a symbol in the novel?
7 What impact can dialogue have on a reader?
8 Give an example of a 'Gothic' element of the novel.
9 What does the horse-chestnut tree symbolise?
10 What do you understand by the term '*Bildungsroman*'?

Tackling the exams

Target your thinking

- What sorts of questions will you have to answer?
- What is the best way for you to plan your answer?
- How can you achieve a high grade?

Your response to a question on *Jane Eyre* will be assessed in a 'closed book' English literature examination. This means that you are not allowed to take a copy of the text into the examination room.

Different examination boards arrange their testing of *Jane Eyre* in different ways, and it is vital that you know on which paper and section the nineteenth-century novel will be, and the sort of question you will face, so that you can be well prepared on the day of the examination.

Marking

The marking of your response will vary depending on the board your school or you have chosen. Each exam board has a slightly different mark scheme, consisting of a ladder of levels. The marks you achieve in each part of the examination will be converted to your final overall grade. Grades are numbered from 1–9, with 9 being the highest.

It is important that you familiarise yourself with the relevant mark scheme(s) for your examination. After all, how can you do well unless you know exactly what is required?

Assessment Objectives for individual assessments are explained in the next section of the guide (p. 83).

Approaching the examination

The suggestions below are relevant for all the exam boards because the boards have so much in common.

- Know the text of the whole novel, not just parts.
- Become familiar with the style and format of the questions on extracts and on the novel as a whole.
- Practise creating plans for answers in five minutes, because you will need to do this in the exam.

- Practise answering questions in the time allowed.
- Learn five to ten really important quotations by heart, and know what points you could make about each.
- Be ready to write about Charlotte Brontë's choice and use of language, and how that language might affect readers.
- Be ready to write about Charlotte Brontë's use of characters, structure or form in a way that conveys your personal response to the novel.
- Refer in your answers to the context in which the novel was written.
- Make sure that you are comfortable using critical terms (e.g. *imagery*, *Bildungsroman* or *genre*), which enable you to write with economy and style.
- Keep in mind the impact on the original readers and how this might be different for readers today.

Timing matters

Once the exam starts you will have about 50 minutes in which to plan and write your answer. The first five to ten minutes are the most important. In that time you analyse the question carefully, work out what it asks you to do and create your plan. In the final few minutes you check that your conclusion relates back to the key point of the question.

What the exam boards have in common

Remember that whichever exam board you are taking, the question will have been designed to assess the objectives set out in the specification. Question styles differ across the boards, as does the arrangement of the Assessment Objectives (AOs) (see 'Assessment Objectives and skills', p. 83).

All four boards assess both AO1 and AO2 in this section of the paper, and all except Edexcel also assess AO3. Always make sure you cover all these AOs in your response, even if they do not seem to be signposted clearly in the question. All questions, except for the second option in OCR, will require you to respond to and analyse a particular passage as well as writing about the novel as a whole. Since you will not know in advance which passage has been chosen, you need to be ready to write about any passage in the novel.

How the exam boards assess *Jane Eyre*

The table below gives you information about where and how *Jane Eyre* is assessed by the different boards.

Exam board	AQA	Edexcel	OCR	WJEC/Eduqas
Paper and section	Paper 1 Section B	Paper 2 Section A	Paper 1 Section B	Paper 2 Section B
Type of question	Extract-based question requiring response to an aspect of the extract and response to the same or similar aspect in the novel as a whole.	Two-part question. Part (a) is based on an extract. Part (b) is a question asking for response to an aspect elsewhere in the text.	Choice of questions. One is extract-based. The other is a discursive essay that requires focus on two 'moments' in the novel.	Extract-based question requiring response to an aspect of the extract and response to the same or similar aspect in the novel as a whole, referring to contexts.
Closed book?	Yes	Yes	Yes	Yes
Choice of question?	No	No	Yes	No
Paper section and length	Paper 1: 1 hour 45 minutes. Section B: approximately 50 minutes.	Paper 2: 2 hours 15 minutes. Section A: 55 minutes.	Paper 1: 2 hours. Section B: 45 minutes.	Paper 2: 2 hours 30 minutes. Section B: approximately 45 minutes.
AOs assessed	AO1 AO2 AO3	Part (a): AO2 Part (b): AO1	AO1 AO2 AO3 AO4	AO1 AO2 AO3
Is AO4 (SPaG) assessed in this section?	No	No	Yes, 5% for this question	No
Percentage of whole grade	20%	25%	25%	20%

Approaching the examination question

First impressions

First, read the whole question and make sure you understand *exactly* what the task requires you to do. It is very easy in the highly pressured atmosphere of the examination room to misread a question – and this can be disastrous. Under no circumstances should you try and twist the question to match the one that you have spent hours revising or the one that you did brilliantly on in your mock exam!

How to read the question

It seems obvious that you need to read the question carefully to make sure you understand what the task requires, but this is not an easy thing to do: reading the question is a complex process. Are you being asked to think about how a character or a theme is being presented? How should language feature in your answer? Make sure you know so that you will be able to sustain your focus later. Look carefully at any bullet points you are given. They are there to help and guide you.

The example below is typical of AQA's style of *Jane Eyre* question and would include an extract (not given here), in this case illustrating Charlotte Brontë's presentation of Rochester. The process of reading the question applies similarly across the boards and has been 'unpacked' for you below.

> Starting with this extract, how does Brontë present Rochester as a sympathetic character?
>
> Write about:
>
> - how Brontë presents Rochester in this extract.
> - how Brontë presents Rochester as a sympathetic character in the novel as a whole.
>
> [30 marks]

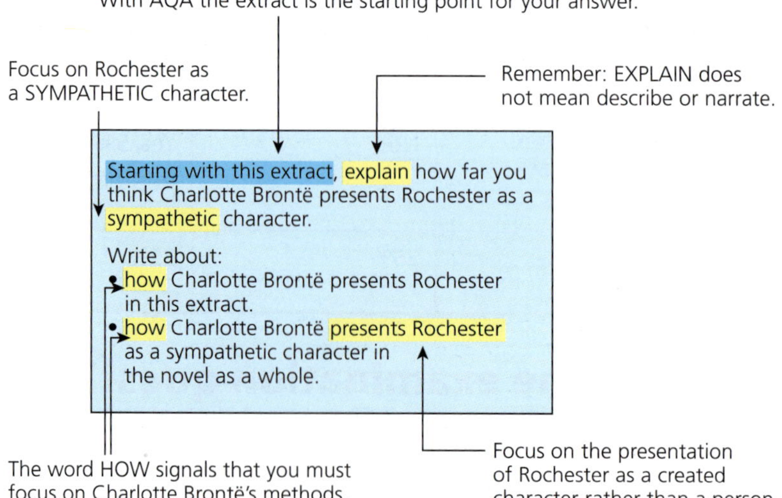

In the exam, as in the example above, it is useful to underline or highlight the key words. They should form the frame for your answer.

There are differences in the ways the exam boards phrase their questions:

- AQA and Eduqas both refer to the 'whole novel'.
- Edexcel uses the phrase 'elsewhere in the novel'.
- Only Eduqas refers directly to 'contexts' in the question.
- Only Edexcel does not assess AO3 (context) in this section.
- Only Edexcel divides its question into two separate sections, a) and b).

Except for OCR, which offers you a choice of questions, all the boards require you to respond to an extract, so once you have read the question your next step is to read the extract very carefully, trying to get an overview or general impression of what is going on, and what or who is being described.

'Working' the text

Now read the passage again, underlining or highlighting any words or short phrases that you think might be related to the focus of the question and are of special interest. For example, they might be surprising, unusual or mysterious. You might have a strong emotional or analytical reaction to them, or you might think that they are particularly clever or noteworthy.

These words or phrases may work together to produce a particular effect, or to get you to think about a particular theme, or to explore the methods the writer uses to present a character in a particular way for his or her own purposes. You may pick out examples of literary techniques such as lists or use of imagery, or sound effects such as alliteration or onomatopoeia. You may spot an unusual word order, sentence construction or use of punctuation. The important thing to remember is that when you start writing you must try to *explain the effects* created by these words, phrases or techniques, and not simply identify them or say what they mean. Above all, ensure that you are answering the question that has been asked.

Planning your answer

Making an essay plan may not earn you any marks but it does enable you to write a better answer, and so improves your chances of a higher grade. There is no standard or expected way to compose a plan – you need to experiment with different ways of planning to find one that suits you. Below are examples of different ways of planning a response to the second bullet in the question above.

Pattern notes, thought mapping, spider diagrams

1 Start with the essence of the question in the centre of your plan.

How Charlotte Brontë presents Rochester as a sympathetic character

2 Think of four or five key ideas and put them around the title.

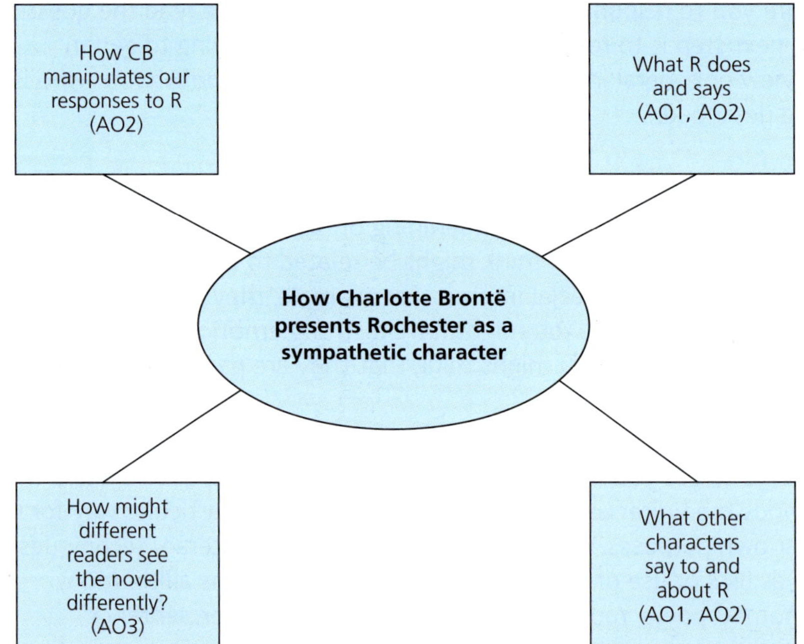

3 Add detailed references and quotations to your key ideas.

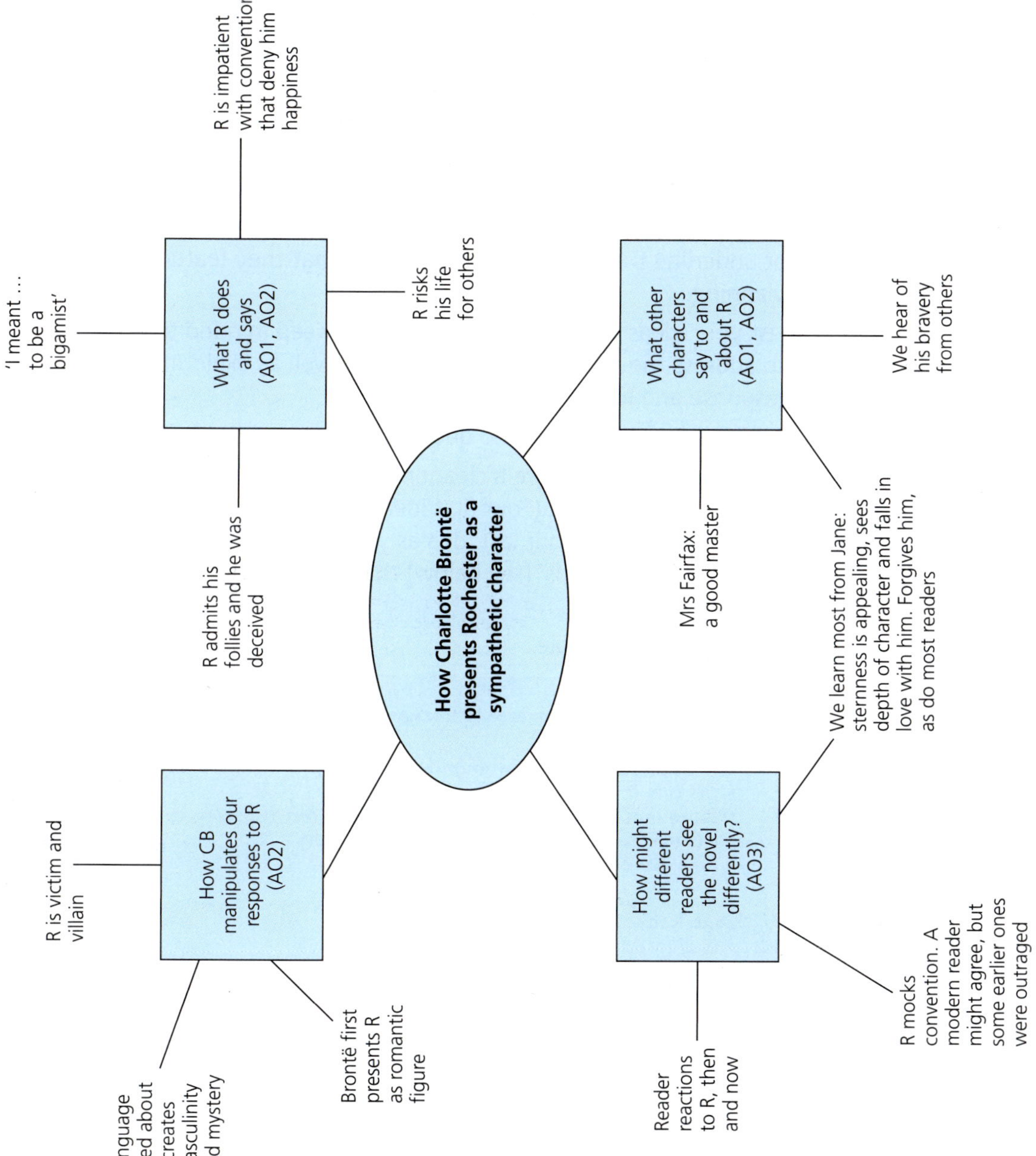

4 When you have mapped out your ideas and the evidence for the points you could make as shown above, decide on the best order for your ideas and major points to make a definite line of argument. There is no need to rewrite your plan – just number the ideas and points in sequence. Start with the best point for an introduction and think how you will conclude with a reference back to the title.

Linear planning

1 Start thinking about your plan as you read the question. Highlight or underline the key terms to make sure that they feature in your planning.

2 List your ideas with space between each. Keep in mind that you need to address the Assessment Objectives as well as exploring your own response and ideas.

3 Add detailed references and quotations to your key ideas.

4 Make sure that you have a clear line of argument and number your key ideas accordingly. (Your first idea might not finish up as your opening point, nor your last idea as your conclusion.) You could write in the 'signpost words' (see below) that link a paragraph with the ones that follow.

See below for an example.

How Charlotte Brontë presents Rochester as a sympathetic character.

a How Charlotte Brontë manipulates our sympathy for Rochester.
- *CB has R as romantic figure.*
- *Language used about R – masculinity and mystery.*
- *CB presents R as victim as well as villain.*
- *Like Jane we grow to appreciate R.*

b What Rochester does and says.
- *R is impatient with conventions.*
- *'I meant ... to be a bigamist.'*
- *R admits follies and recounts how deceived.*
- *R risks his life for others.*

c What other characters say to and about Rochester.
- *We learn most from Jane: sternness is appealing, sees depth of character and falls in love with him. When she forgives him, so do most readers.*
- *We hear of his bravery from others.*
- *Mrs Fairfax says he is a good master.*

d How different readers might see the novel differently.
- *Reactions of readers, then and now, to R.*
- *R mocks convention. A modern reader might agree, but some earlier ones outraged.*

Whichever style of planning you prefer, once you have planned out what you want to say you can concentrate on saying it well.

How to make your argument clear

Try to make sure that the examiner can see what you were thinking by reading what you have written. To help do this, signpost your line of argument by using terms and phrases such as:

- Firstly
- although
- consequently
- nevertheless
- but the original readers might have felt...
- however
- On the other hand
- An alternative view would be that...
- Finally

You should say what you think, so don't be afraid to write 'I think that...'; merely asserting your personal point of view will not gain you many marks, however. You always need to cite evidence from the novel for the points you make and then go on to explore and analyse that evidence (see 'Sample essays' on p. 89 for examples of answers that do this).

GRADE BOOSTER

Never lose sight of the author in your essay. Remember that *Jane Eyre* is a construct - the characters, their thoughts, their words, their actions have all been created by Charlotte Brontë - so most of your points need to be about what she might have been trying to achieve. In explaining how her ideas are conveyed to you, for instance through an event, something about a character, the use of symbolism, personification, irony and so on, don't forget to mention her name. For example:

- Charlotte Brontë makes it clear that...
- It is evident from ... that Charlotte Brontë is inviting the reader to consider...
- Here, the reader may well feel that Charlotte Brontë is suggesting...

How to use quotations

Except when writing about an extract that is before you on the exam paper, you can use quotations only if you can remember them. That alone should convince you that short quotations are better than long ones, but there are other good reasons for keeping quotations brief. Short quotations are better because they:

- are quick to write down
- can clinch your point quickly
- leave you time to explore your ideas
- gain as much credit as longer quotations
- reveal your knowledge of the novel rapidly
- show that you can select judiciously from the text

Rather than trying to remember long quotations it is easier, and more effective, to remember key words and/or very short phrases and use these 'mini quotations' to clinch the points you make.

Look through the (long) quotations below and try to select from them 'mini quotations' (key words or short phrases) that you could use to fill in the blanks in the paragraph about St John Rivers that follows.

> Thinking aloud about Rosamond: 'If I offered my heart, I believe you would accept it. But that heart is already laid on a sacred altar: the fire is arranged round it.'
>
> (p. 424)

> 'Reason, and not feeling, is my guide: my ambition is unlimited; my desire to rise higher, to do more than others, insatiable.'
>
> (p. 432)

> 'The humanities and amenities of life had no attraction for him – its peaceful enjoyments no charm. Literally, he lived only to aspire.'
>
> (p. 453)

> 'There are no such things as marble kisses or ice kisses, or I should say my ecclesiastical cousin's salute belonged to one of these classes; but there may be experiment kisses, and his was an experiment kiss.'
>
> (p. 459)

> 'God and nature intended you for a missionary's wife. It is not personal, but mental endowments they have given you: you are formed for labour, not for love. A missionary's wife you must – shall be.'
>
> (p. 464)

St John Rivers is a complex character who has a complicated relationship with his faith and with other people. In Diana's words, he is 'a strange being.' Although he is initially shown as a handsome, intelligent and appealing figure when he offers Jane hospitality, the reader increasingly senses his flinty lack of feeling. It is no surprise when he declares '________________.' His lack of humanity is evident when he resists his own affection for Rosamond Oliver because his '________________.' His restlessness of spirit is kept under control by his ambition: he says '________________' and this shows his dedication to be selfish rather than selfless. As for his capacity for loving – there is a coldness about him that Jane feels is almost tangible in his '________________.' He seems unaware of the impact of telling Jane that '________________.' She later comments that if they were to marry, 'you would kill me.'

It can also help to practise writing paragraphs on two or three different examples of the effect of language in a particular passage. Realistically this is what you would have time to write about in the exam.

Writing in an appropriate style

Remember that you are expected to write in a suitable *register*. This means that you need to use an appropriate style. This means:

- *not* using colloquial language or slang, e.g. 'John Reed is a nasty piece of work. A bit of a toe-rag really.' (The only exception is when quoting directly from the text.)
- *not* becoming too personal, e.g. 'Bessie is like my mate, right, 'cos she...'
- using suitable phrases for an academic essay, e.g. 'It could be argued that', not 'I reckon that...'
- *not* being too dogmatic – don't say 'This means that...'; it is much better to say 'This might suggest that...'.

You are also expected to be able to use a range of technical terms correctly. If you can't remember the correct name for a technique but can still describe its effect, you should still go ahead and do so.

Using the last minutes well

The last thing that an examiner reads before deciding on your mark is usually your final paragraph. That means that you have the opportunity to confirm in the examiner's mind that you:

- have understood and responded relevantly to the question
- have developed a line of argument

- know the novel well (not as a film)
- appreciate how Charlotte Brontë has used language and structure
- are aware of the nineteenth-century context
- realise that readers respond differently
- can write fluently in an appropriate critical style

You cannot do everything listed above in one paragraph. You can, however, be aware of what you have written before and cover any obvious gaps with a brief reference or comment. You can also look back at the question and refer back to its key terms in your concluding sentences.

GRADE BOOSTER

Below is a list of popular ways to waste time in an examination. **Avoid them!**

- Telling the story of the novel, even though the examiners know well what happens.
- Writing out long quotations, which gain you no more marks than short quotations.
- Picking out literary features ('this is a metaphor') without exploring their impact on the reader.
- Saying what you think without providing any textual evidence to back up your opinion.
- Criticising Charlotte Brontë as boring.

How to raise your grade

The most important advice is to answer the question that is in front of you, and to start doing so promptly. When writing essays in other subjects, you may have been taught to write a lengthy, elegant introduction explaining what you are about to do. You have only a short time in the literature examination, though, so it is best to get started as soon as you have gathered your thoughts together and made a brief plan.

Students often ask how long their answer should be. It is difficult to give a definitive answer because candidates have different-sized handwriting, but quality is always more important than quantity. A strongly focused answer of 2–3 pages that hits the criteria in the mark scheme will be rewarded at the very highest level. Conversely, a response that is 6–7 pages long but not focused on the question will not receive many marks at all.

Be careful to avoid lapsing into narrative or simply retelling the story because most questions are essentially about the author's methods, not about what happens or whom the characters are. If you are asked about how Charlotte Brontë presents Mr Rochester, remember that the focus of the question is about the methods that Charlotte Brontë uses. Do not simply tell the examiner what Mr Rochester does or what he is like; this is a very common mistake.

Remember that, except for OCR's second option, you need to write about the extract but also to deal with the focus of the question in the novel as a whole, or in the case of Edexcel, 'elsewhere in the novel'. You will be penalised if you do not do this, so you *must* keep an eye on the clock and leave time for writing about the novel as a whole. If you feel you have more to offer in terms of comments on the extract, leave a space so that you can return to it if necessary.

GRADE *FOCUS*

Grade 5

- Candidates have a clear focus on the text and the task and are able to 'read between the lines'.
- Candidates develop a clear understanding of the ways in which writers use language, form and structure to create effects for the readers.
- Candidates use a range of detailed textual evidence to support comments.
- Candidates use understanding of the idea that both writers and readers may be influenced by where, when and why a text is produced.

Grade 8

- Candidates produce a consistently convincing, informed response to a range of meanings and ideas within the text.
- Candidates use ideas that are well linked and often build on one another.
- Candidates dig deep into the text, examining, exploring and evaluating the writer's use of language, form and structure.
- Candidates carefully select finely judged textual references that are well integrated in order to support and develop responses to texts.
- Candidates show perceptive understanding of how contexts shape texts and responses to texts.

Achieving a Grade 9

To reach the very highest level you need to have thought about the novel more deeply and produced a response that is conceptualised, critical and exploratory at a deeper level. You might, for instance, challenge accepted critical views in evaluating whether the writer has always been successful. If, for example, you think Charlotte Brontë set out to create indignation over the plight of women, how successful do you think she has been?

You need to make original points clearly and succinctly and to convince the examiner that your viewpoint is really your own, and a valid one, with constant and careful reference to the text. This will be aided by the use of short and apposite (really relevant) quotations, skilfully embedded in your answer along the way (see 'Sample essays', p. 89).

REVIEW YOUR LEARNING

(Answers are given on p. 110.)

1 Which exam paper will include *Jane Eyre*?
2 Can you take a copy of *Jane Eyre* into the exam?
3 Which Assessment Objectives are tested through *Jane Eyre*?
4 How long will you have to answer the *Jane Eyre* question?
5 Have you understood how you are expected to respond to extracts and to the novel as a whole?
6 Which type of planning suits you best?
7 Why are short quotations more useful than long ones?
8 Give examples of 'signpost' words you find useful.
9 How can you make good use of the last few minutes of the exam?
10 Do you always have to write a full answer when practising timed answers?

Assessment Objectives and skills

All GCSE English literature courses are designed to assess how well you read, understand and respond to literary texts. Most of *what* is to be assessed and *how* it is to be assessed has been specified at national level through what are known as Assessment Objectives (AOs). This explains why the exam boards have such similar approaches. Nevertheless, there are some variations in the way literature is assessed so you need to check the table below to make sure that you know how the board you will be sitting has framed the assessment of *Jane Eyre*.

Assessment Objectives

AO1 Read, understand and respond to texts. Students should be able to:

- maintain a critical style and develop an informed personal response
- use textual references, including quotations, to support and illustrate interpretations. (35–40%)

AO2 Analyse the language, form and structure used by a writer to create meanings and effects, using relevant subject terminology where appropriate. (40–45%)

AO3 Show understanding of the relationship between texts and the contexts in which they were written. (15–20%)

AO4 Use a range of vocabulary and sentence structures for clarity, purpose and effect, with accurate spelling and punctuation. (5%)

As you will see from these national weightings, the two Assessment Objectives that carry the most marks are AO2, analysing a writer's methods (i.e. language, form and structure), and AO1, developing your personal response. Showing that you understand how the context relates to the text, if it is assessed through the *Jane Eyre* question, carries fewer marks, and the accuracy with which you write carries a maximum of 5 per cent for this question. That does not mean that some of the Assessment Objectives do not matter – you need every mark you can get – but it does mean that you need to prepare yourself as thoroughly as possible to write about your response to the novel and to analyse Charlotte Brontë's methods.

The table below shows which Assessment Objectives are examined via the *Jane Eyre* question by the different boards.

AQA	Edexcel	OCR	WJEC/Eduqas
AO1	AO1	AO1	AO1
AO2	AO2	AO2	AO2
AO3		AO3	AO3
		AO4	

What skills do you need to show?

There is no secret about how to do well on the *Jane Eyre* question. You just need to demonstrate the skills that the examiners are looking for, which are outlined in the Assessment Objectives. Below is an explanation in student-speak of what the examiner-speak of the Assessment Objectives really means.

AO1 Read, understand and respond to texts. Students should be able to:

- maintain a critical style and develop an informed personal response
- use textual references, including quotations, to support and illustrate interpretations.

At its most basic level, this AO is about having a good grasp of what a text is about and being able to express an opinion about it within the context of the question. For example, if you were to say, 'The novel is about the love between Jane Eyre and Rochester', you would be beginning to address AO1 because you have made a personal response.

The word '**develop**' tells you that it is not enough to scribble down points as they occur to you. You need to build an argument, based on evidence, which is a clear response to the task set. An '**informed**' response refers to the basis on which you make that response. In other words, you need to show that you know the novel well enough to answer the question.

AO1 also requires you to '**use textual references, including quotations, to support and illustrate interpretations**'. This means giving short direct quotations from the text (as suggested in 'Tackling the exams', pp. 78–79), and where possible embedding them in the flow of your answer. Quotations on their own do not gain marks – they need to be there because they offer support for your developing line of argument. Sometimes it is better to refer to an event than to give a quotation. For example, it is easier to refer to Jane's return to Gateshead Hall to see

Mrs Reed than to find a quotation showing that she did return. Do make sure, though, that you include some direct quotations to address this objective, even if they are from the extract itself.

Generally speaking, most candidates find AO1 relatively easy. Remember that you are writing for an examiner – someone you do not know, but who knows *Jane Eyre* well and will expect to read responses in Standard English.

Avoid retelling the story – there are no marks for doing that. Storytelling signals to the examiner that you do not realise that '**a critical style**' means offering thoughts and opinions about a text, rather than just saying what happens in the text.

AO2 Analyse the language, form and structure used by a writer to create meanings and effects, using relevant subject terminology where appropriate.

This AO focuses on how Charlotte Brontë as a writer communicates her meanings to the reader. Most examiners would probably agree that covering AO2 is a weakness for many candidates, particularly those students who only ever write about the characters as if they were real people.

- **Language:** 'language' encompasses a wide range of writer's methods, such as the use of different types of imagery, words that create sound effects, similes, irony, and so on. AO2 also refers to your use of '**subject terminology**'. This means that you should be able to use terms such as 'metaphor', 'alliteration' and 'hyperbole' with confidence and understanding. If you can't remember the term, don't despair – you can still gain marks for explaining the effects being created. The best way to gain high marks on almost any literature question is to write well about specific words that the author chose to use and their likely impact on readers. For example, when Jane is finally returning to Thornfield the short sentences and fractured phrasing reveal her emotion: 'Could I but see him! ... I cannot tell – I am not certain. And if I did – what then?' (p. 488).
- **Form:** you need to keep in mind that Charlotte Brontë was writing a novel with readers in mind, and to refer to this whenever appropriate. 'Form' includes the narrative viewpoint, and with *Jane Eyre* Charlotte Brontë's choice of a first-person narrative style is particularly important.
- **Structure:** this is about the novel's construction: why the events are in the sequence they are in; how themes feature; why events happen

as they do and how the plot is built up. For example, the novel is built around Jane's journeys – each major section ends or begins with a journey. Another example is the way there are continual references to thematic ideas – at the end Adèle is rescued from an unsuitable school and this reminds readers of Jane's experience at Lowood and therefore of how education has featured as a theme throughout the novel.

- **Use relevant subject terminology:** this part of AO2 is about the economy and effectiveness of your writing. Imagine that you are writing for your English teacher and use some of the key critical terms that he or she has taught your class (e.g. 'context', 'imagery' or – if you want to show that you know – '***Bildungsroman***'). Such terms are a 'shorthand' to scaffold your ideas, to make your writing more economical and give it greater precision.

Bildungsroman: a novel about the moral and psychological growth of the main character.

AO3 Show understanding of the relationship between texts and the contexts in which they were written.

'**Context**' is a word with multiple meanings, which are unpicked for you in the 'Context' section (p. 11).

This AO is about how time and place affect writers and readers. It means that you need to show that you know when the novel was written and how the fact that Charlotte Brontë was writing in the mid-nineteenth century might have influenced how she wrote. You might also consider literary context (how Charlotte Brontë's reading influenced her writing) and the personal context of her own life.

AO3 also means demonstrating that you understand how the original readers might have reacted and how their reactions might have differed from those of modern readers (for example, over the presentation of religion in the novel).

AO4 Use a range of vocabulary and sentence structures for clarity, purpose and effect, with accurate spelling and punctuation.

The way you write does matter. As examiners read your response they form impressions of the mind behind your words. You want your examiner to sense that you use and interpret words well. It is possible for a candidate to think well but write badly, but you might be surprised how rarely that happens. An examiner under time pressure (and they are) might not stay patient with an illegible script or might undervalue a badly written one.

How can you prepare for meeting the AOs?

Below are ways of making it second nature to address the Assessment Objectives in your writing:

- Working with a partner, look at a range of questions on *Jane Eyre* from past papers and try to identify which AOs are targeted. (Check with your teacher if you can.)
- It takes only five minutes to create a plan, so do plenty of them as practice. Develop the habit of planning your responses with the AOs as part of your planning process, and highlight parts of your plan in different colours to check that the different AOs are covered.
- Practise timed answers until you know the AOs by heart.

How do questions assess the AOs?

In the AQA-style example below, the way in which questions target the Assessment Objectives has been indicated.

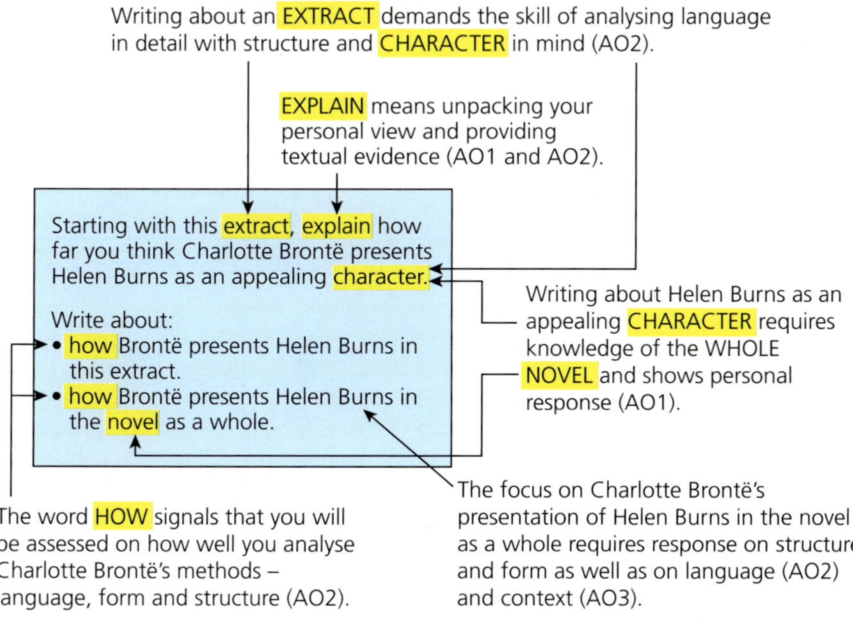

GRADE BOOSTER

Building your written response in the exam around the Assessment Objectives is not the key to gaining the highest grades. That approach may be given credit for its coverage but not for its creativity or originality. Instead, try to offer a convincingly personal response that includes demonstrating the skills and knowledge assessed by the objectives. Practise enough for it to become automatic to address language, form, structure and context, so that you can concentrate on how your argument answers the task.

REVIEW YOUR LEARNING

(Answers are given on p. 110.)

1. Which Assessment Objectives does your board assess through the question on *Jane Eyre*?
2. Which Assessment Objectives usually carry the most marks?
3. What does AO1 assess?
4. What does AO2 assess?
5. What does AO3 assess? (If your board assesses AO3 through *Jane Eyre*.)
6. What does AO4 assess? (If your board assesses AO4 through *Jane Eyre*.)
7. What might you do to help you tackle the AO you find most challenging?

Sample essays

Target your thinking

- What type of question will you face on *Jane Eyre* in your GCSE English literature examination?
- What are examiners looking for when they assess your work?
- What are the features of Grade 8 and Grade 5 answers?
- What does a well-structured essay look like?
- What is the most effective way to use quotations and textual references?

Thinking about sample questions and answers is a good way to get your head round what examiners give marks for. Assessing sample answers against your board's criteria will help you to assess your own practice answers.

Before reading any more of this section, make sure that you have read 'Tackling the exams' on how to plan and write answers and 'Assessment Objectives and skills' on how to understand the Assessment Objectives.

Bear in mind that most boards require you to write in detail about an extract from *Jane Eyre* **and** to write more generally about the novel as a whole. AQA assesses your answers together, but some boards assess skills differently in the different parts of their questions.

Below are two answers to the same question. The question is in AQA style, but the evidence that gains marks is similar across the boards.

Question 1

Read the following extract from Chapter 27 of *Jane Eyre* and then answer the question that follows.

At this point in the novel Mr Rochester has tried to persuade Jane to live with him unmarried.

...while he spoke my very conscience and reason turned traitors against me, and charged me with crime in resisting him. They spoke almost as loud as Feeling: and that clamoured wildly. "Oh, comply!" it said. "Think of his misery; think of his danger; look at his state when left alone; remember his headlong nature: consider the recklessness following on despair – soothe him; save him; love him; tell him you love him and will be his. Who in the world cares for *you*? or who will be injured by what you do?"

Still indomitable was the reply: "*I* care for myself. The more solitary, the more friendless, the more unsustained I am, the more I will respect myself. I will keep the law given by God; sanctioned by man. I will hold to the principles received by me when I was sane, and not mad – as I am now. Laws and principles are not for the times when there is no temptation: they are for such moments as this, when body and soul rise in mutiny against their rigour; stringent are they; inviolate they shall be. If at my individual convenience I might break them, what would be their worth? They have a worth – so I have always believed; and if I cannot believe it now, it is because I am insane – quite insane: with my veins running fire, and my heart beating faster than I can count its throbs. Preconceived opinions, foregone determinations, are all I have at this hour to stand by: there I plant my foot."

I did. Mr Rochester, reading my countenance, saw I had done so.

Starting with this extract, how does Charlotte Brontë present Jane Eyre as an independent-minded woman?

Write about:

- how Charlotte Brontë presents Jane in this extract.
- how Charlotte Brontë presents Jane's independence of mind in the novel as a whole.

[30 marks]

[AO4 (4 marks)]

You will see below extracts from exam responses from two students working at different levels. They cover much the same points. If you look carefully, however, you will be able to see how Student Y takes similar material to that of Student X, but develops it further in order to achieve a higher grade.

Student X, who is likely to achieve Grade 5, begins the response like this:

I am going to explain how Charlotte Brontë presents Jane in the extract and then how she presents her in the novel as a whole. The extract comes after the marriage has been stopped and Bertha has been revealed in her madness. Jane is responding to Mr Rochester's desperate plea to her to run away with him to the south of France.

There is a kind of conversation in her own head about the pros and cons of becoming Mr Rochester's mistress. She also thinks how little anyone else cares about what she does, and so what does it matter anyway? The other side of the argument is put by her independence of mind – a sort of mixture of principles and pride. She says to herself that the more 'unsustained' she is, the more she will respect herself, even if no one else does. She also thinks that she has God on her side because marriage is sacred.

1 Repeating the question gains no marks. This paragraph shows knowledge of the text but not much more.

2 Shows insight supported by references from across the text, but short on quotations as evidence.

3 Some use of quotation, but tends to assert rather than prove the points made.

This is a promising start and would suggest that Student X is working at Grade 5 and demonstrating 'clear understanding'. The response is well focused on the task and there is implicit awareness of Charlotte Brontë's methods and their effects on the reader, though these are not fully explained and there is a tendency to summarise rather than analyse.

A better response appears next. Student Y is working at Grade 8. Look carefully and see if you can identify the differences between the two responses.

Student Y, who is likely to achieve Grade 8, begins like this:

The extract comes at a pivotal point in the novel as an unprecedented affirmation of Jane's independence of mind. Charlotte Brontë's narrative voice, moving from dialogue to reflection and back again, helps to make that independence of mind apparent. At one point the pseudo-autobiographical narrator even asks herself, 'Who in the world cares for you? or who will be injured by what you do?' This makes it clear that Jane's dilemma is of her own making, but the more passionate her love for Mr Rochester the more the reader is invited to admire the strength of mind with which she resists his attempt to make her his mistress. The struggle within her is between her head – her moral duty – and her heart or 'Feeling'. Her conscience does not give the obvious, virtuous advice not to go, but 'traitorously' argues that to leave Rochester would be criminal. This suggests to the reader just how painful her internal struggle is.

1 Immediate, analytical address to the question, with focus on the author's methods and fluent use of subject terminology.

2 Analysis of the use of particular words and their effect on the reader.

3 Comment on author's methods and awareness of readers.

4 Exploration of character with detailed analysis and awareness of reader.

Student Y's introduction is stylishly accomplished and shows intelligent grasp of authorial intentions and techniques. There is evident awareness of likely reader reactions.

Having launched their essays effectively, although at different levels of sophistication, both students go on to engage with the question in relation to the extract and then widen their answers to include the whole novel.

Student X writes:

Jane uses grand-sounding words but then she makes her position plain – 'there I plant my foot.' To keep her ground despite Mr Rochester seeming to devour her with his 'flaming glance' is real independence of mind.

There is a pattern in the way she turns down marriage proposals for her own reasons. It is touch and go whether or not she will give in to St John Rivers and marry him.

We should not be too surprised by Jane's refusals, because she has always been very independent-minded. At Gateshead Hall she resists John Reed's attack on her and has the nerve to tell Mrs Reed what she thinks of her unjust treatment of her. At Lowood she resents Mr Brocklehurst, and although she has to do what she is told, as readers we know what she thinks of him and his hypocrisy.

1 Some analysis of language and exploration of effect.

2 Awareness of structure with reference beyond the extract, but there is little textual evidence or analysis.

3 Comments show awareness of impact, but are insufficiently located in textual evidence.

Student Y writes:

Charlotte Brontë gives Jane two motives to oppose the passionate flood of feeling for Rochester. One is her self-respect: –'I care for myself. The more solitary, the more friendless, the more unsustained I am, the more I will respect myself.' The other is her religious belief in the sanctity of marriage: 'I will keep the law given by God; sanctioned by man.' Jane is capable of telling herself that, 'Laws and principles are not for the times when there is no temptation: they are for such moments as this.' In doing so she is not spouting received religious wisdom – her belief is personal, individual and an indicator of her sense of self and her independence of mind.

Charlotte Brontë reveals Jane's internal struggle through the language she uses. She says all she has are 'preconceived opinions, foregone

1 Effective analysis of the character as construct, clinched with apt quotation.

determinations' and the polysyllabic abstractions ring rather hollow, but then her deeper determination comes through as she makes her position almost physical with simple metaphoric monosyllables – 'there I plant my foot.' No wonder Rochester later exclaims, 'never was anything at once so frail and so indomitable.'

Jane's independence of mind emerges early in the novel as she rebels against the tyranny of John Reed. She fights her first independent-minded battle against the unfairness of Mrs Reed, feeling in her passion that, 'Speak I must: I had been trodden on severely, and must turn.' That refusal to accept the unjust or unreasonable is apparent at Lowood when she (unlike Helen) boils with indignation over Helen's unfair treatment by Miss Scatcherd and burns the placard that had been hung round Helen's neck. It is her independence of mind that enables her to acquit herself with such dignity at Thornfield, when coping calmly with Mr Rochester's questions in a way that 'not three in three thousand' young schoolgirl-governesses could manage. She has the independence of mind to see through the shallow pretentiousness of the guests at Thornfield – when she describes Blanche Ingram as sitting 'in queenly amplitude' the adjective 'queenly' is resonant with overtones of self-regard and social snobbery. It is another sign of that independence that she can be subjected to the pressure of the eloquence of St John Rivers, yet declare simply but strongly, 'I feel I have adequate cause to be happy, and I will be happy. Good-bye!' and refuse to marry him.

2 Effective analysis of language in relation to character and ideas.

3 Interpretation supported by quotation.

4 Relevant response, based on textual reference and showing understanding of events, theme and ideas.

5 Convincing character analysis, based on detailed textual evidence.

The conclusions of the two answers cover similar territory but differ in the way they cover it. Student X's conclusion is relevant and shows genuine engagement with the novel but focuses at the level of character:

> *It is Jane's independence of mind, very unusual for a woman in Victorian times, that gives her the strength to resist St John Rivers because his idea of love does not match her own. It is part of her appeal to the reader, and to Mr Rochester, who does not want a subservient slave girl.*

1 Apt, if brief, reference to Victorian attitudes towards women.

Student Y's conclusion focuses more on the writer, is shaped more effectively in relation to the question and finishes on a stylishly intelligent note:

> *As a young woman of independent means and mind, Jane defies conventional expectations and marries maimed Rochester, but nothing demonstrates her independence of mind more than the episode in the extract. At a moment when she risked being carried away on a flood of passionate feeling, when the flames of Rochester's passion were about to devour her, she still possessed her own soul and her own sense of being an independent woman, making her own decisions: 'I am a free human being with an independent will, which I now exert to leave you.'*
>
> *As Charlotte Brontë has her tell the reader, Rochester did not marry her – she married him.*

1 Awareness of what society expected of young women in Jane's position. Appreciation of historical and literary context.

2 Shaped conclusion showing insight into the author's methods in terms of characters, ideas and structure.

Sample answer X

This answer is uneven but it has definite strengths. It would just gain Grade 5 because, although it starts with summary and contains little explicit mention of the author, there is clear understanding of some of Charlotte Brontë's methods and a convincing, detailed engagement with the text. With a more effective opening, more sophisticated expression and deeper analysis this response would gain a higher grade.

Sample answer Y

This answer would merit Grade 8 since it is fluently written and digs deeply into the text, examining and evaluating the writer's use of language, form and structure and offering a range of interesting interpretations. It sustains focus on the task, conveys ideas with coherence and uses an appropriate register.

It shows a secure understanding of key aspects of the text, with considerable engagement, supporting and justifying responses by direct reference to the text, including quotations. It explores beyond the surface, offering informed insights and convincingly personal ideas.

Question 2

The following extracts from sample responses are based on an extract-based question that focuses on a theme, rather than a character. The format for the question is broadly as for Eduqas, but is similar to questions set by the other boards (except one option for OCR) in that it requires you to consider both an extract and the novel as a whole.

You should use the extract below and your knowledge of the whole novel to answer this question.

Write about how religion is presented at different points in the novel.

In your response you should:

- refer to the extract and the novel as a whole
- show your understanding of ideas, characters and events in the novel
- refer to the contexts of the novel.

[40 marks]

"Humility, Jane," said he, "is the ground-work of Christian virtues: you say right that you are not fit for the work. Who is fit for it? Or who, that ever was truly called, believed himself worthy of the summons? I, for instance, am but dust and ashes. With St Paul, I acknowledge myself the chiefest of sinners; but I do not suffer this sense of my personal vileness to daunt me. I know my Leader: that He is just as well as mighty; and while He has chosen a feeble instrument to perform a great task, He will, from the boundless stores of His providence, supply the inadequacy of the means to the end. Think like me, Jane – trust like me. It is the Rock of Ages I ask you to lean on: do not doubt but it will bear the weight of your human weakness."

> "I do not understand a missionary life: I have never studied missionary labours."
>
> "There I, humble as I am, can give you the aid you want: I can set you your task from hour to hour; stand by you always; help you from moment to moment. This I could do in the beginning: soon (for I know your powers) you would be as strong and apt as myself, and would not require my help."

Student X, who is hoping to achieve Grade 5, begins like this:

> *Charlotte Brontë makes religion an important theme throughout the novel, particularly so when Jane meets St John Rivers, who is speaking for most of the extract. He is trying to persuade Jane to join him in India as a missionary's wife. He acknowledges himself as 'the chiefest of sinners' but he is not really humble. He is trying to take the life of another – Jane – to serve his purpose of gaining a 'mansion in heaven' through being a great missionary. When he asks the question, 'who, that ever was truly called, believed himself worthy of the summons?' we know that the answer is himself.*

1 Puts the extract briefly into context, showing knowledge of events in the novel.

2 Analysis of the use and effect of particular words.

3 Exploration of character, linked with analysis of language.

This opening paragraph has definite strengths and, although it makes only a brief reference to the author, would be worthy of a Grade 5: it shows understanding of the situation and begins to analyse language in relation to character.

The response by Student Y does all of that, and more, in a strong opening paragraph:

> *The image of religion that Charlotte Brontë conveys in this extract is one of hypocrisy overlaid with humility. When St John acknowledges himself as 'the chiefest of sinners' and talks of his 'personal vileness', we know as readers that he is not truly humble – the word 'I' occurs five times in the final paragraph alone, signalling his egocentric attitude. He has great confidence and as he says, his 'ambition is unlimited.' He is sure enough of himself to try to take the life of another – Jane – to serve his purpose of gaining a 'mansion' in heaven through missionary dedication and achievement. When he asks the rhetorical question, 'who, that ever was truly called, believed himself worthy of the summons?' we know that the answer is himself, the man strong enough to resist the earthly lure of beautiful, doting Rosamond Oliver for the sake of a higher calling, which for him means eternal recognition.*

1 Immediate, analytical address of the question with awareness of Charlotte Brontë's intentions.

2 Incorporation of relevant quotation from beyond the extract.

3 Embedded support for the exploration of character, with analysis of language using appropriate subject terminology.

Student Y writes concisely and fluently, using an appropriate critical register. The response engages rapidly with Charlotte Brontë's authorial intentions and draws on the text to prove the points made. There is awareness and analysis of the impact of characters' words.

The answer from Student X continues with a level of comment that would gain Grade 5 because it shows understanding of character and events and engages in some detail with language and its impact. Quotations are incorporated effectively into the line of argument:

> *St John Rivers is a powerful preacher, and it shows here in the extract: there is a biblical ring about 'I know my Leader: that he is just as well as mighty.' However behind that biblical language is a cold-hearted character. St John Rivers proves to be lacking in human warmth. Jane's brief, simple response contrasts with St John's eloquence and this makes us recognise the differences between them.*
>
> *Charlotte Brontë's attitude to religion is established early on in the novel – Mr Brocklehurst is a Christian hypocrite who treats the girls in Lowood appallingly. He is at his most hypocritical when he tells Miss Temple off for giving the girls bread and cheese instead of inedible burnt porridge because it would 'starve their immortal souls.'*

1 Comment on author's methods and awareness of the impact of words on readers.

2 Comment on the contrast between words and characters.

3 Moving into considering the novel as a whole.

4 Comment on language in relation to character and ideas.

Student Y continues to write stylishly and confidently, referring appropriately to the historical context and drawing on evidence from across the novel:

> *We know that St John's sermons are powerfully eloquent and his eloquence is visible in the extract: there is a soaring biblical rhetoric about 'I know my Leader: that he is just as well as mighty … It is the Rock of Ages I ask you to lean on.' However behind that rhetoric is the icy, rock-like character that Charlotte Brontë has created to embody the hardness and hollowness at the heart of official religion. St John Rivers proves to be a cold Evangelical, lacking in human warmth and secretly despising his 'fellow worms.' Jane's brief, simple and human response is in complete contrast to St John's self-conscious eloquence. This helps us recognise that the linguistic gulf between them is matched by an emotional gulf.*

1 Confident comment on author's methods with awareness of readers.

2 Apposite quotation to clinch point.

3 Analysis of the impact of language on readers.

Charlotte Brontë's attitude to religion is established early on in the novel – Mr Brocklehurst is the embodiment of Christian hypocrisy. His treatment of Lowood girls is anything but charitable and his shaming of Jane is sadistic. There is bitter irony in the comment from the saintly Helen Burns that he is a clergyman and 'said to do a great deal of good.' He is at his most viciously hypocritical when he criticises Miss Temple for giving the girls bread and cheese instead of the inedible burnt porridge because it would 'starve their immortal souls.' No wonder contemporary readers challenged the novel Jane Eyre as 'anti-Christian' despite its ending with the words 'Jesus Christ.'

4 Appreciation of historical and literary context.

Both answers conclude with final paragraphs that are relevant and fluently written.

Student X concludes with:

There are many positive images of religion throughout the novel. Jane frequently refers to God, and refuses to break the sanctity of marriage by becoming Rochester's mistress. Even Rochester finally seeks 'reconcilement to my Maker.' Charlotte Brontë seems to suggest that personal belief is what matters, not organised religion with its hypocritical representatives who talk of God but think only of themselves.

1 Valid comment but at the level of summary rather than analysis.

2 Relevant response to question, based on textual evidence and showing understanding of events, theme and ideas.

Student Y's conclusion does all of the above, and more:

Nevertheless, Charlotte Brontë has seeded positive images of religion throughout the novel. Helen Burns for example can cope with the prospect of an early death because she believes that 'life is so soon over, and death is so certain an entrance to happiness – to glory.' Jane herself frequently refers to God, and seeks to do his will. This is most obvious when she refuses to break the sanctity of marriage by becoming Rochester's mistress – 'I will keep the law given by God; sanctioned by man.' It is also seen when she wanders (like Christ in the wilderness?) for days without food or shelter and 'felt the might and strength of God.' Even Rochester, formerly 'an irreligious dog' by his own admission, finally (but for some readers not entirely convincingly) seeks 'reconcilement to my Maker.' Charlotte Brontë's presentation of religion seems to suggest that personal belief is what matters, as exemplified in Jane, not organised religion with its representatives who speak of God but use religion to cloak their self-interest.

1 Interpretation supported by quotation.

2 Relevant response to question, based on textual evidence and showing understanding of events, theme and ideas.

3 Confident, stylish and accurate expression in a conclusion that relates directly to the question.

Sample answer X

This response shows insight when commenting on the writer's presentation of the theme through language, form and structure. It sustains focus on the task, conveys ideas coherently and uses an appropriate register. It shows a secure understanding of key aspects of the text, with considerable engagement, supporting and justifying responses by direct reference to the text, including quotations. Overall, a Grade 5 is achieved.

Sample answer Y

This response concludes more strongly, supports points more effectively with textual evidence, and shows a sensitive awareness of a writer at work and recognition that reader responses may vary. Detailed analysis of the use and effect of particular words is deployed effectively. There is an intelligent tentativeness about some of the interpretation and deliberate reference back to the question. A Grade 8 is clearly deserved here.

Top quotations

As your examination will be 'closed book' and you will have only a short extract in front of you, you might find it helpful to memorise some quotations to use in support of your points in the examination response, particularly when addressing the question in relation to the rest of the novel. See the 'Tackling the exams' section on p. 69 for further information about the format of the examination.

You don't need to remember long quotations; short quotes that you can embed into a sentence will be more effective. If all else fails and you find that you can't remember a full quotation, try to remember its main message – as long as you can remember the gist of what the quotation relates to, you can use a textual reference. For example, instead of the first quotation below, you might say that John Reed's character was revealed through his unpleasant appearance and his stupidity.

The following quotations can be used as a quick reminder of the ways that Charlotte Brontë presents key characteristics of the main characters, of her main themes and of her techniques as a novelist.

Top ten characterisation quotations

1 John Reed was 'large and stout for his age, with a dingy and unwholesome skin ... not quick either of vision or conception' (p. 12)

- A typically crisp analysis of John Reed's character, as shown through his appearance and stupidity.

2 Mr Brocklehurst is 'a black pillar! ... the grim face at the top was like a carved mask, placed above the shaft by way of capital.' (p. 38)

- The simile emphasises the stony hardness of Mr Brocklehurst, who looms over Jane like a column from a temple.

3 Helen Burns has 'the aspect of an angel' (p. 80)

- Helen's focus on the life to come is often reflected in the way she is described.

4 Helen Burns on Jane: 'you are too impulsive, too vehement.' (p. 82)

- This description, from a friend, echoes what others like Mrs Reed have said about Jane being too passionate.

5

Jane declares to Mr Rochester that it is as if 'we stood at God's feet, equal – as we are!' (p. 292)

- Jane's view of their equality is matched by Rochester's and presented as important by the author.

6

'I meant ... to be a bigamist; but fate has out-manoeuvred me.' (p. 336)

- Rochester's defiance of convention would have outraged many of the original readers, who viewed marriage as sacred.

7

'I will keep the law given by God; sanctioned by man.' (p. 365)

- This is Jane's firm and fixed position, despite her passionate love for Rochester.

8

St John Rivers: 'Reason, and not feeling, is my guide: my ambition is unlimited.' (p. 432)

- This devastating self-analysis explains why Jane feels that marriage to St John Rivers would 'kill' her.

9

St John Rivers: 'human affections and sympathies have a most powerful hold on you' (p. 409)

- A justified comment on Jane's capacity for emotion.

10

'Am I hideous, Jane?'
'Very, sir; you always were, you know.' (p. 505)

- A wonderful exchange that encapsulates the relationship between Jane and Rochester.

GRADE BOOSTER

The memory part of your brain loves colour! Try copying these quotations using different colours for different characters. You might organise them into mind maps, or write them on to sticky notes and put them up around your room. Flash cards can also be fun and effective if you can enlist the help of a partner.
Another useful method is to record quotations on to your mp3 player and play them over and over. Or you might try watching one of the many film adaptations to spot where a quote appears. This can be an effective method as you have both sound and vision to help you and you can see the quotation in context.

Top ten thematic quotations

1 Mr Brocklehurst: 'Humility is a Christian grace' (p. 41)

- An early signal to the reader that religious attitudes and pretensions will feature in the novel.

2 Mr Brocklehurst: 'you may indeed feed their vile bodies, but you little think how you starve their immortal souls!' (p. 75)

- The best example of the religious hypocrisy that so outraged Charlotte Brontë.

3 Helen Burns: 'I believe; I have faith: I am going to God.' (p. 97)

- Helen exemplifies how belief can enable human beings to endure a difficult life or anticipated death.

4 Jane: 'Laws and principles are not for the times when there is no temptation…' (p. 365)

- This is a positive affirmation of principled belief on Jane's part.

5 Of Miss Temple: 'She had stood me in the stead of mother, governess, and, latterly, companion.' (p. 100)

- Jane's comment embodies a view of education that is about caring and respect – the reverse of everything Mr Brocklehurst embodies.

6 'Women feel just as men feel; they need exercise for their faculties, and a field for their efforts as much as their brothers do.' (p. 129)

- Charlotte Brontë felt so strongly about the way in which women were treated as second-class citizens that she gave Jane the same attitudes as herself.

7 'I am a free human being with an independent will, which I now exert to leave you.' (p. 293)

- As this indicates, Charlotte Brontë created Jane as an example of an independent-minded woman.

8 Jane: 'Not a human being that ever lived could wish to be loved better than I was loved.' (p. 363)

- The love between Jane and Rochester has a passionate intensity – exactly what Charlotte Brontë believed was necessary as a basis for marriage.

Rochester: 'Station! station! – your station is in my heart, and on the necks of those who would insult you, now or hereafter.' (p. 304) 9

- Rochester's indignation here emphasises that Jane's rise from poor, orphaned governess to be the beloved of an aristocrat was part of Charlotte Brontë's critique of society's falseness.

Rochester: 'My bride is here ... because my equal is here, and my likeness. Jane, will you marry me?' (p. 294) 10

- This quotation encapsulates the author's view of love and of society.

GRADE BOOSTER

The most frequently used method for learning quotations is to write them down, repeat them and then test yourself. If you are a visual learner, however, you might try drawing one of these quotes, with the quotation as a caption.

Top writer's methods quotations

Of Gateshead Hall: 'the cold winter wind had brought with it clouds so sombre, and a rain so penetrating...' (p. 9) 1

- Charlotte Brontë often uses pathetic fallacy – having the weather reflect human experiences – as she does here, since the weather is as pitiless as the Reed family.

'Oh Aunt! have pity! Forgive me! I cannot endure it...' 2
'Silence! This violence is almost repulsive.' (p. 22)

- The use of dialogue heightens the intensity of a moment, as here when Jane is forced back into the red room.

'What a miserable little poltroon had fear, engendered of unjust punishment, made of me in those days!' (p. 38) 3

- Much of the story is told by Jane as an older woman, looking back on her earlier experiences.

'A new chapter in a novel is something like a new scene in a play; and when I draw up the curtains this time, reader, you must fancy you see a room in the George Inn at Millcote.' (p. 111) 4

- Charlotte Brontë makes Jane a self-conscious narrator, in conversation with the reader.

5 'Here then I was in the third story, fastened into one of its mystic cells; night around me; a pale and bloody spectacle under my eyes and hands; a murderess hardly separated from me by a single door.' (p. 242)

- Charlotte Brontë consciously includes 'Gothic' elements in her story.

6 'I loved him very much – more than I could trust myself to say – more than words had power to express.' (p. 304)

- When she chose to, Charlotte Brontë wrote very simply and clearly, as here.

7 Jane, at the prospect of leaving Rochester: 'a hand of fiery iron grasped my vitals' (p. 363)

- Charlotte Brontë uses a powerful metaphor to suggest the intensity of Jane's passionate love for Rochester.

8 Rochester: 'I am no better than the old lightning-struck chestnut-tree.' (p. 512)

- Charlotte Brontë uses a symbol – the old chestnut tree – as a signal to the reader of what will happen and what has happened on the human level.

9 About blinded Rochester: 'And reader, do you think I feared him in his blind ferocity? – if you do, you little know me.' (p. 498)

- Here Charlotte Brontë continues the fiction that Jane is the narrator of her own life story.

10 'Reader, I married him.' (p. 517)

- Deservedly the most famous quotation in the novel, this sentence uses word order to affirm the power of the woman – it is Jane who does the marrying.

Wider reading

Literary critical works and articles

This is a list of literary critical works and articles that you might find useful for wider reading around *Jane Eyre*. It is presented in rough order of difficulty. Always ask yourself whether the time spent reading criticism might be better spent reading the novel itself.

- Jane O'Neill: *The World of the Brontës* (Carlton Press, 1997)
- Sarah Rowbotham: *Jane Eyre* (York Notes, 2002)
- Jess Kadow: *A Guide to the Classics – Jane Eyre* (The Student Review, 2011)
- Q.D. Leavis: the Introduction to the Penguin edition of *Jane Eyre* (first published in 1966 but full of valuable insights and analysis)
- Sara Lodge: *Charlotte Brontë – Jane Eyre: A Reader's Guide to Essential Criticism* (Palgrave Macmillan, 2008)
- Harold Bloom: *Charlotte Brontë's Jane Eyre – Modern Critical Interpretations* (Chelsea House, 1986)

Useful websites

- www.cliffsnotes.com/literature – detailed and informative notes on *Jane Eyre*, including summary as well as analysis.
- http://crossref-it.info – offers information and activities on *Jane Eyre* that are useful for GCSE.

Other resources

- Should you have the opportunity, a visit to Haworth and the Brontë Parsonage would give you an insight into how and where Charlotte Brontë lived.

Answers

Answers to the 'Review your learning' sections.

Context (p. 19)

1 Social, historical and literary factors that influenced Charlotte Brontë's thinking, including events in her own life.
2 Cowan Bridge School.
3 Charlotte Brontë's sister Maria.
4 Clergyman.
5 Governess.
6 Selfish, foolish and unworthy of any kind of admiration.
7 A genuine believer, but sceptical about organised religion and angered by religious hypocrisy.
8 Jane defends the rights of women to be independent.
9 Mystery, atmospheric houses/settings, controlling characters, sensational events, blood and darkness.
10 Not necessarily – the novel suggests that rank does not matter but that personal qualities do, which may mean that Jane is more conventional than her creator.

Plot and structure (p. 36)

1 Gateshead Hall, Lowood School, Thornfield Hall, Moor House/Morton and Ferndean.
2 Because Mr Reed, her uncle, requested it on his deathbed.
3 This was the room where Mr Reed died, and it seems haunted.
4 His hypocrisy is exposed by the way he spoils his daughters.
5 Mr John Reed is mentioned earlier in the novel.
6 Eerie atmosphere and references to myth and mystery.
7 Through Jane's caustic comments and their own words.
8 Jane is made to reject it because it breaks God's law.
9 St John's emotional ice versus Rochester's fiery passion.
10 Decide how satisfying you find it – there is no correct answer.

Characterisation (p. 48)

1 Bessie Lee.
2 Helen Burns.
3 How he spoils his daughters compared with his treatment of the girls at Lowood.
4 Explicit comments from Rochester, his behaviour towards Blanche and his valuing of Jane.
5 Jane's descriptions dismiss Blanche as shallow, and Blanche's comments and conduct prove this.
6 There is no 'correct' view – trust your personal reaction.
7 Rochester and St John Rivers; Jane and Blanche Ingram; Eliza and Georgiana Reed.
8 Initially impressed, she is increasingly aware of his icy ambition and heartlessness.
9 By having Jane comment directly to the reader on her continuing devotion: she has never cared for appearance.
10 The ending is almost too good to be true, but what matters is what you think of it.

Themes (p. 57)

1 An idea developed throughout a novel.
2 Education, religion, romantic love, the role of women.
3 Through Jane's experiences of learning at Gateshead Hall.
4 Gateshead Hall, Lowood School, Thornfield Hall, Morton.
5 Through Mr Brocklehurst.
6 Mr Brocklehurst, Helen Burns, St John Rivers and Jane herself.
7 Fire, the chestnut tree, the sea.
8 By refusing to be bullied or controlled by anyone – John Reed, Mrs Reed, Mr Brocklehurst, Rochester or St John Rivers.
9 Selfish, spiteful, vain and vacuous.
10 Comment through Jane's words and her character.

Language, style and analysis (p. 68)

1 Autobiography.
2 Immediacy and control of the reader's perspective.
3 John Reed's outward ugliness suggests inner rottenness, but this is not so with all characters – Rochester's forbidding appearance belies his inner sensitivity, for instance.

4 She uses pathetic fallacy, where the weather reflects emotional states, e.g. the 'cold winter wind' at Gateshead Hall, the storm at Thornfield.
5 There is no absolute pattern, but some names for people reflect their qualities – feeble Reeds, feverish Burns and awe-inspiring Temple.
6 Fire is literal (Thornfield) and emotional (the fire of passion).
7 It makes the reader into a listener, giving greater immediacy.
8 The atmosphere and noises on the third floor of Thornfield Hall.
9 The love between Jane and Rochester.
10 A coming-of-age novel.

Tackling the exams (p. 82)

1 This depends on which board you are taking. Check the table in 'How the exam boards assess *Jane Eyre*' (p. 71).
2 No.
3 This depends on which board you are taking. Check the table in 'How the exam boards assess *Jane Eyre*' (p. 71).
4 Usually 45–50 minutes.
5 Only you will know, but check with your teacher.
6 Try out different approaches and decide for yourself.
7 They are easier to remember, quicker to write and more effective.
8 Look through your own practice answers to find out.
9 See 'Using the last minutes well' (pp. 79–80).
10 No – writing a plan rather than a full answer may be more useful.

Assessment Objectives and skills (p. 88)

1 Check the table in 'Tackling the exams' (p. 71).
2 AO1 and AO2.
3 AO1 assesses your personal response to the text and its content.
4 AO2 assesses what methods/techniques Charlotte Brontë has used and their effect on readers.
5 AO3 assesses personal, historical and literary context.
6 AO4 assesses the accuracy and effectiveness of your writing.
7 Check with your teacher.